PENGUIN BOOKS

The Book of Fame

Lloyd Jones is the author of the controversial *Biografi*, a travel book set in Albania in Communism's aftermath. *Biografi* was published in New Zealand, Britain, the United States and Germany and judged one of the best books of the year by the *New York Times*. His short stories have been published in New Zealand and overseas; the collection *Swimming to Australia* was shortlisted for the New Zealand Book Awards. Lloyd Jones' most recent novel, the provocative and disturbing *Choo Woo*, was published in New Zealand and Australia to critical acclaim. Jones met his American wife Jo-Ellen in Greece; they have three children and live in Wellington.

The Book of Fame

Lloyd Jones

PENGUIN BOOKS

PENGUIN BOOKS

Penguin Books (NZ) Ltd, cnr Airborne and Rosedale Roads, Albany,
Auckland 1310, New Zealand
Penguin Books Ltd, 80 Strand, London WC2R 0RL, England
Penguin Putnam Inc, 375 Hudson Street, New York, NY 10014, United States
Penguin Books Australia Ltd, 487 Maroondah Highway,
Ringwood, Australia 3134
Penguin Books Canada Ltd, 10 Alcorn Avenue, Toronto,
Ontario, Canada M4V 3B2
Penguin Books (South Africa) Pty Ltd, 5 Watkins Street,
Denver Ext 4, 2094, South Africa
Penguin Books India (P) Ltd, 11, Community Centre,
Panchsheel Park, New Delhi 110017, India
Penguin Books Ltd, Registered Offices: Harmondsworth, Middlesex, England

First published by Penguin Books (NZ) Ltd, 2000
This edition published 2001

3 5 7 9 10 8 6 4 2

Copyright © Lloyd Jones 2000

Editorial services by Michael Gifkins and Associates

The right of Lloyd Jones to be identified as the author of this work in terms of
section 96 of the Copyright Act 1994 is hereby asserted.

Designed by Mary Egan
Typeset by Egan-Reid Ltd, Auckland
Printed in Australia by McPherson's Printing Group

www.penguin.co.nz

one   getting to know one another   7

two   making a name for ourselves   27

three   fame's arrow   49

four   how we think   69

five   homesickness   77

six   fatigue and the irresistible attraction of defeat   101

seven   overseas experience   131

eight   off the record   165

         afterthoughts   175

         acknowledgements   177

There was no holy water
No one spoke of fame
There were no reliable works

We were left to figure out things for ourselves

one

getting to
know one
another

one

There were twenty-seven in our party. Besides George Dixon, our manager, and Jimmy Duncan, coach —

Billy Stead was a bootmaker

Bob Deans, a farmer

Bunny Abbott, a farrier and professional runner

Dave Gallaher, a meatworks foreman

Billy 'Carbine' Wallace, a foundryman

Jimmy Hunter farmed in Mangamahu, north-east of Wanganui

Fred 'Fats' Newton

'Massa' Johnston

Jimmy O'Sullivan

Bill Cunningham was a miner

Frank Glasgow, a bank officer

George 'Bubs' Tyler, swimmer & boatbuilder

Steve Casey

Simon Mynott

Eric Harper, farmer

George Smith, former jockey, professional runner

George Gillett

Freddy Roberts

Mona Thompson, a civil servant

Duncan McGregor

George Nicholson was a blacksmith & bootmaker

Bill Mackrell
Billy Glenn, farmer
Ernest Booth
Bill Corbett, miner
Alec McDonald
& Charlie 'Bronco' Seeling

◆

8 August, 1905
A crowd of one hundred braved the sleet and cold to see us off. We stood by with our luggage and football boots, our collars turned up against the weather, aboard the SS *Rimutaka*, and slowly like a big log wedged then freeing itself mid-stream, our lives came round to port then stern, then out to the Heads, whereupon the tugs dipped their flags; and clinging together the tug men gathered on the foredeck with their farewell song. The wind tore away the last line of 'Auld Lang Syne', the tugs dropped out of sight, and after that we hit out on our own.

◆

We were Aucklanders, some Otago and Taranaki boys, a few Cantabs and Wellingtonians; Stead was a lone Southlander, Corbett a sole West Coaster, and Hunter came out of a place near Wanganui with a Maori name in which every sound spoke of bush-creeping isolation. The larger sense of who we were hadn't yet forged itself. But in small telling ways, through gesture and anecdote, we revealed ourselves to one another —
The bookworm in Billy Stead
Mona Thompson's fondness for setting his hat brim at a low tilt
Eric Harper's learned ways with cutlery and table napkins
Dave Gallaher's passion for cards
Jimmy Hunter's habit of closing his eyes and touching his nose whenever praised

George Nicholson's singing

Cunningham's singing and Frank Glasgow's piano playing; it only took a snatch of a melody from Cunningham for Frank to produce the whole works

Bob Deans' pious ways; his knocking on our cabin doors to rally up a respectable showing for evening chapel

The devotion of Bill Corbett and Fats Newton to breakfast

The way George Tyler would butter his toast and afterwards, lick each finger tip

Cunningham's love of shovelling coal into the stoker

Seeling's refusal to do the same

The lags and wisecrack artists emerged

The sleepers — Mackrell, McGregor, Glasgow

Those who were early to bed and jovial and spry at breakfast

Bubs Tyler's tale of a man he knew who got his kneecap bitten off after a large shark thought to be dead was paraded through the dance hall in Tauranga

Those to whom a story was turned over, stone by stone, as if seeking evidence of the 'true and false' variety — Was the shark dead? How long had it been out of the water? — and others who sat back and enjoyed it like music.

Second day out we got on with our shipboard training —
'Blind boxing'
'Pillow fighting'
'Chalking the deck'
Cricket with other passengers and crew
Us against 'the world'
We won that, then turned the ship's rigging into an obstacle course

We divided the ship and took the lower deck for a 'training field' — jogging sprinting

dribbling

and congregated on the upper deck using it as a 'classroom' for

ball skills

scrum work

& passing rushes

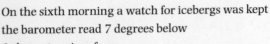

On the sixth morning a watch for icebergs was kept

the barometer read 7 degrees below

& the water pipes froze

We were 800 miles south of Bluff

We passed a pod of whales, their sides covered in barnacles

The skies turned to thin glass and it grew steadily colder

Billy Stead stayed up one night to catch an iceberg 'in its luminous haze . . . quiet, mystic, not a sound of progress . . .'

In the morning cold rain and hail drove us indoors, and kept us there; day and night, lanterns swayed in the creaking dark.

We were studying lit diagrams in our laps and George Tyler had put forward his 'shark story' to illustrate the value of 'surprise in unexpected places' when the wind chopped round to the south-west and a sea struck on the starboard quarter, right against our cabins, with tremendous force.

Portholes were shot through with ocean spray; cabins flooded; some had to pick themselves off the floor.

In the saloon we waded knee-deep in water.

In the smoking lounge, thirty-two feet above sea level, the skylights, strutted with iron bars, broke like matchsticks.

Glass ashtrays washed across the timber floors.

George Nicholson kicked at the spume, yelling at it, 'Go on, get outa here!' Mister Dixon shook his head. 'Fruitless, George, talking back at the sea like that.'

Bill Mackrell, who wasn't feeling well, simply climbed to a higher bunk.

The upper deck received a giant wave and the chef, carrying a bag of flour and a dish of raisins, fell breaking three ribs.

There was a moment when the storm stopped to catch its breath and the skipper and chief engineer said it was the worst storm they'd known, not ever, but since 1893; and that year, 247 wrecks were reported in a single night in the English Channel. Shipwreck? It hadn't entered our minds until that moment.

The storm passed and we ventured out on deck to an oyster-grey world. The seas were a grey slop with long traces of spittle.

We looked around and found ourselves walled in by ocean and sky.

We were the only ones out on deck and it was an unpleasant surprise to find ourselves so alone. There were five women in our saloon but we wouldn't see them again until we'd rounded the Horn and, by then, come in to shirt-sleeves weather. At that moment all of us seemed to know this, and we hunched our shoulders and tried not to look too closely into one another's cold faces.

Being nowhere in particular, and without traditions to adhere to, we could be whatever or whoever we chose.

At night, awake in his bunk, Bill Cunningham struggled to conjure up 'the pick 'n' shovel' rhythm of his miner's life — already it felt distant, like a place inhabited by cousins once visited as a child. While you've never gone back you can't forget it either.

He turned his head on his pillow to the oiled walls inches away from his nose.

Mining is forever squeezing yourself into tighter spaces.

At sea, you expand. You develop wings. You lift off.

At sea, you can be anything.

So there he is, dressed up as Neptune,

a 'minstrel', and once or twice, even as a woman,

tottering back and forth to Fred Glasgow on piano.

With whole days to kill we found ourselves discovering and favouring one part or another of the ship —

the crafted vee where ship rail meets ship rail to divide the ocean, the homeward drift of the black funnel smoke.

We were in danger of going our separate ways until Mister Dixon called us together. While we packed our pipes we listened to him propose that, from now on, all knowledge and experience would be pooled. Tomorrow morning we should come into the world as if we had no prior knowledge of it. We should wake up and proceed looking afresh and start the naming process over.

In this way we renamed the stars. On the following nights we tried to remember where we had put them.

Mister Dixon scratched his chin. We were almost there, but not quite, he said. He was more anxious to create 'an atmosphere' where we might share and share alike. Tobacco. Stories. Whatever we happened to carry in our pockets or in our thoughts. 'Let's crack open that treasure and share ...' In this spirit, those who had wives and girlfriends at home found themselves donating small descriptive features to the men who didn't, thus allowing them to construct and furnish their own visions.

To get the ball rolling Mister Dixon spoke of Mrs Dixon: '... her tsarina pose, chin raised ...' As we watched, Mister Dixon's placid eyes appeared to fade and drift away from us. 'I've got her in my sights now. It's a Sunday afternoon and she's lying along the couch with a book, sun streaming in the window.'

'... the line of her mouth tightening, eye sparkling ... Sometimes,' says Gallaher, 'I'd think she was holding back something.'

'... on Saturdays she'd wear a blue bow in her hair. And I'd say, "Hallo, look who's come gift-wrapped ..."' Duncan McGregor raised his eyebrows and hands as if to ask, 'Will that do? It's all I've got.'

George Smith mumbled into the mid-distance, '... her hips moving under her dresses ...'

'. . . a face containing a kind of forbidden language. Eyes blue, dark background, crooked teeth . . .' We all looked Simon Mynott's way; the balding sections of his head shone in the ceiling light. We were interested to pursue that theme. But Bob Deans brought us back on track with: '. . . picking blackberries, a light mist on her chin and throat . . . shadows in her white cotton shirt . . . Her name was Natasha. It was her name I liked best, I think.'

'. . . long black dresses, her white shirt sleeves rolled up, a riff of dark hair on the arms . . .' Massa Johnston sat upright, his arms crossed in an air of matter-of-factness.

'. . . just walking along, saying nothing, our elbows, arms touching . . .' (Deans)

'. . . chestnut hair . . . I can tell you it was genuine chestnut. More than that I won't say . . .' (Simon Mynott, again)

'. . . ears tipped with cleverness . . .' (Jimmy Duncan)

'. . . her teeth a gorgeous rabble . . .' (O'Sullivan)

'. . . you saw her bare shoulder and you thought of a low and narrow doorway. I understand her grandparents are from Dalmatia . . .' (Massa)

'. . . left foot trailing over stern on the Wanganui River . . . and all along bellbirds calling to us.' (Jimmy Hunter)

'. . . the way she'd get out of the bath — collecting herself in her arms . . .' (George Smith)

'. . . and all of a sudden she'd say, "Pull in here, Jimmy."' (Jimmy Hunter)

'. . . nibbling of your lips like a sparrow . . .' (O'Sullivan)

Then George Smith mentioned 'her salmon-coloured lips'
and everyone fell quiet.

◆

On the thirteenth day we saw the snow-clad hills of Tierra del Fuego.
The snow melt, and the dark solid bits that held it together. Well, it
was a thing of beauty. In our football kit we stood up to the ship rail
and in a single glimpse we rediscovered our taste for land. Tyler jokingly
threatened to swim ashore. Then Cunningham took control. Turning
his back on Tierra del Fuego he clapped his hands and called for
another scrum to be put down.

In calm seas we rounded the Horn. During the warmest part of the
day, we placed our cheeks against the deck where the sun preserved
itself in salt and paint.

Two days later, Massa Johnston and Frank Glasgow hauled the piano
out on deck and sang 'Rowsy Dowsy Girls' to celebrate the re-
emergence of the five women from our saloon.

As the weather got warmer, the piano thawed and began to leak. At
night a seabird would walk across its keys, and George Nicholson lay
in his bunk ticking off the notes — E flat, and that, I believe, is F sharp.

Now we saw flying fish cut across our bow. George Tyler grinned down
at the gossipy pattern they left on the water. 'Hallo you,' he'd say to a
fish with butterfly fins.

Two days later, we found ourselves steaming across a fishing ground.
We leant over the rail picking out fish and their small darting shadows.
From the stern, Dave Gallaher and Jimmy Duncan threw out baited
lines and brought in Cape Pigeons and Mollymawks to entertain
the ladies.

One morning the land rose out of the sea. It looked startlingly near. We stared back at it trying to make up our minds about South America. The Otago boys were reminded of the coast around Timaru — a rough outline of life, cattle grazing over green slopes, clouds moving off the hilltops.

Montevideo. Our first experience of a foreign city. We went ashore, Carbine with his camera to photograph the monuments.

Cunningham bought an alligator egg, and Smith some primitive carvings.

Jimmy Duncan complained of the locals speaking Spanish and making no bloody attempt at English, and on top of that — which he found the worst aspect — they acted like they'd never heard of it.
Likewise Roberts who asked for a cup of tea.
'You know — tea?'
But it was pointless.

That night, in the glow of an oil lamp, Stead began a letter home.
'Imagine everybody in Invercargill using garlic and onions for every meal, and cobblestones sticking up at every kind of angle and hawkers hawking anything from brooms to livers, all exposed to air . . .'

That was Montevideo. None of us liked its foreignness and open sewer pits. But we were there to take on coal and passengers. We lent over the ship rail feeling possessive of our little ship.

A man ran up the gangway, his paintbrushes tipping out the open end of a canvas bag.
Some Indians wrapped in old blankets and with the faces of ghosts waded up the gangway like it was a mountain path; a Frenchman in a white suit and white boater with a snakeskin hat band oversaw the loading of a number of cages containing native parrots bound for a circus entrepreneur in Europe.

getting to know one another

These passengers and cargo were followed by Bob Deans. We cheered him aboard. Bob had been out to buy a dozen hard young pumpkins for the backs to hone their passing skills.

Off the coast of Uruguay, Jimmy Duncan called for a practice. We set up a drive; performed some dribbling and passing skills.

The next morning we lined up to face Brazil and practise our haka. Among the onlookers, a group of Uruguayan women in white pinafores and parasols.

◆

The nights were now warm and clear and we met on the upper deck to debate football matters. The angle of the scrum. The formation of the backs. Billy Stead and Fred Roberts arranged the pumpkins on the deck and we stood over them with our pipes, debating possible lines of attack. Billy convinced us to embrace the idea that everything we did on the field must have as its end design 'the creation of space'. Time and again we re-arranged the pumpkins and determined to find new ways through. The ways were seemingly endless.

Mister Dixon distanced himself from these discussions. He sat in a deckchair compiling thoughts and observations to write down in his diary.

'Warmer weather as we go north. Chief Engineer took some snapshots of Heaven. Cunningham's knowledge of scrumwork proving invaluable.

Aug 23. Most of us are stripped down to our football togs all day.

Aug 29. Hottest day yet. Not a breath of wind and the sea is gluey. Passed a shoal of porpoises . . .

Crossed the Equator this morning and immediately changed course
out to the Atlantic . . .'

That evening we gathered up the pumpkins to make space to dance.
Mister Dixon handed out dance cards. In addition to the piano, we
had a violin and piccolo orchestra. There were only six ladies to go
round, plus Cunningham in fancy dress; the rest of us danced with
dummies. On the stroke of midnight Jimmy Duncan gave each of us a
gentle shoulder-tap reminder that we had training in the morning,
and one by one we sloped back to our bunks to swap notes.

getting to know one another

MONA THOMPSON'S DANCE CARD

Dances	Partners
Grand March	farmer's wife, mother of
Waltz	'Teresa' (I think). Picked her glove up from the deck. Brown quail-like freckles on breast
Lancers	blue dress one, almond eyes pretty scar tissue beneath left eye
Waltz	Massa Johnston's honey
Barn Dance	blonde Venezuelan whose laughter we hear during dinner
Polka	'Anna'? drew llama on Jimmy Hunter's menu
Waltz	Senorita Boa. At 'debates' said the word for story and history is the same in German and Mister Dixon got involved
Lancers	'Cecilia'? yellow ribbon, lemur wrap, glassy eyes & teeth
Waltz	Teresa

◆

'September 1. In hot humid conditions we held the finals of the sports
events —
Harper and Hunter, a dead heat in the potato race
Glasgow, the pillow fight

Booth, the sack race
Thompson, the obstacle course
Mynott, quoits
Hunter, arm wrestling
Gallaher, "chalking the deck"'

◆

Tenerife. Blessed land. In Santa Cruz we took a ball ashore. Freddy
Roberts persuaded a number of Arab fig vendors to form a line and
oppose us in lineout drill. Cunningham jumped well, secured good
ball.

Jimmy Duncan got everyone to pull on a face plate and swim out to
the reef to watch the shoal behaviour of fish.

We filled ourselves with fruit, then it was back out to the Atlantic.

◆

For a fancy costume ball hosted by the passengers of the First Saloon,
Nicholson dressed as a tramp, Newton as a 'disreputable working
woman', Tyler as a 'nigger minstrel', Cunningham as Chief Steward,
Harper a gaucho, Thompson as the strongman, Eugene Sandow;
Glasgow showed up as a tattooed warrior, Mackrell and Roberts as
clowns. Nicholson's costume won him first prize.

'September 4. Weather cooler. Everyone training vigorously except
O'Sullivan, down with sunstroke.
Counting the days now.
September 5. Passed Cape Finisterre.'

◆

Close to forty days we'd been at sea. We developed a morbid shipboard stare, hanging off the rails, gazing down as though into our very graves.

We had forgotten the point of newspapers. We stopped talking as if none of that mattered either. Players withdrew, the big men to a ledge deep inside themselves. Nicholson, 'the song bird', fell quiet.

At our lowest ebb England answered. She sent out signals that she was near. The seas thickened with fishing boats and marker buoys. Late in the day, a large cruiser steamed by in the opposite direction to ourselves. We ran to that side of the ship and waved but no one waved back. Casey said he saw a woman with a cocktail drink in a gloved hand.

That last night at sea we sat up late writing postcards of Arabs and pyramids we'd bought in Tenerife ready to send home the moment we stepped ashore.

Before dawn the boys were up on deck, leaning against the rails, smoking their pipes. In the darkness we bumped into one another —
'Gidday farmer'
'That you, Bunny?'
'No, it's your mother . . .'
'Jimmy, what are you doing up?'
We were embarrassed to be found so wanting.

Crouched by an oil lamp Eric Harper concluded his letter: 'The English shores are in sight and the excitement is too great to continue . . .'

In the dark, England came to us in a series of noises —
Foghorns. Ships' whistles. Hissing.
We strained to make her out. None of us spoke. Each of us entertained a private notion of what England should be like.
'There she is . . .' Mister Dixon it was.

getting to know one another

Anyway we all looked. And there she was!

England. A crane poking through the fog. Now the rest of England passed through the hole in the fog — rooftops, beyond them the dark shadows of hills. Within those shadows, outlines of cottages, roofs. The view began to jam and our eyes raced from one piece of the jigsaw to the next.

We tried to locate something of what our parents had said, or a vista passed down by our grandparents.

One or two of the players argued with the view. 'No, that's not right . . .'

The woman from the cake shop in Cuba Street had told Billy Wallace to expect English roses. For forty days at sea he had been preparing himself for a botanic experience.

England was a muddled picture to start with. We found ourselves trying to disassemble what we saw from what we knew or had heard or read of a storybook past — the sound of horses, their shocking emergence out of the mist, famous wars, heaths and witches' brew.

A coal hulk came into view and immediately a homely knowledge descended over Corbett.

Jimmy Duncan needlessly reminded Tyler, 'That's England, son . . .' and Tyler looked for the tower he had only seen illustrated in *Dick Whittington and his Cat.*

A seagull's cry reminded Cunningham of all the lonely coasts he's known, the place of dreams.

In the emerging light Dave Gallaher looked back for the Plymouth headland, that shaven bit that meets the sea that we passed in the dark. It could be North Head at the entrance to the Manukau.

Johnston's expression is one of disapproval. He's just seen three men struggling with a box and calculates that it should only take two men to carry it. The third one, he figures, is bluffing.

Smith, the former jockey, glances up. The sky comes and goes. He looks down at the grey sea and feels a shooting sensation in his heart.

Mister Dixon is all smiles as he mentally composes a letter to his 'Dear Emma . . .'

Alec McDonald, at someone's insistence, scrutinises a brick building and winces as someone else insists: 'No, but really, it's different from ours . . .'

There is a sound of wood on wood as the tender brushes alongside the SS *Rimutaka*. At that moment Bunny Abbott hears doors creaking in the bush — he blinks — and seeing it's England, colour enters his cheeks. A hunter's excitement catches in his throat. He swears quietly to himself.

'Aha! There!' Deans points to the first spire.

Glasgow is first to smell England's old, official air — something like leakage from a five-pound note.

Freddy Roberts juggles the ball in his hands. He can't wait to get on land.

Mackrell holds back a hacking cough behind a closed hand in case the English might hear and get the wrong impression.

The artist from Uruguay points out to Mona Thompson a different palette. He can identify some of the colours, but not all. 'That, for example,' he says of the grey light.

The O in O'Sullivan's mouth is pronounced — he has the muddled idea that he's been here before.

Jimmy Hunter stares into the fog, thinking how mid-morning around Wanganui on an autumn's day, the hills are suddenly dreamt into existence.

Seeling switches his weight from foot to foot, nodding blindly whenever something of interest is pointed out.

The slightly wounded look developed at sea shows no sign of leaving Steve Casey. A whole itinerary of places are lodged in his face — beginning with lonely icebergs, the unknown wilds of Patagonia, festering Montevideo and palmy Tenerife.

Elsewhere on deck, as more passengers emerge, there is the silent mutter of folk arriving inside a library or museum. You hear each one say, 'Oh look, England.'

The smiles shift from Mister Dixon's face. A sudden surge of managerial responsibility sees him button his collar. Who knows what is awaiting them down on the wharf? He wonders whether he should blow his nose now or save it for later. He sniffs.

A brass band strikes up and Billy Stead immediately removes his hands from his pockets.
This is it then. This is where we've come to play.

◆

Bob Deans gathered up all the pumpkins and in the space cleared we clustered around Mister Dixon for a final talk on deportment. 'There are just one or two things I have to say on this matter and others. Primarily, I suppose, about how best to represent your country. Questions, dilemmas will arise. For example, which look to present?

Which foot to lead with? Is this smile for me or for my country?' His advice, in the end, was to the point. We should just be ourselves. 'Right, then,' he said. 'Any questions?'

So this was what we were supposed to feel. We adjusted our ties and drew encouragement from Mister Dixon's confident manner — 'This way, boys,' and with our luggage grips and boots we tripped down the gangway to board the tender. Once the last of us were accounted for the passengers up on deck raised three cheers. We responded with a haka.

The good folk of Plymouth slept on.

We'd left New Zealand in hail and sleet to arrive in England in near darkness. As we stepped ashore a voice from the dark said, 'Welcome to England.' It was a reporter wanting a word with Mister Dixon and Dave Gallaher 'if possible?' That was Mister Dixon's first managerial decision. It came as a surprise (unusually for him) and we saw him scratch his chin. 'I see no reason why not,' he said. Encouraged, other pad-and-pencil men emerged. A photographer arranged us. Freddy Roberts found a football. The first English photograph finds us in high spirits, Fred balancing the ball on the end of his fingertips, half a mind to pass it on once the photographer is finished and put Billy Wallace away. There was a flash! and Fred flicked the ball behind his head, George Smith took it and in the same motion shot it round his back to Jimmy Hunter who, without lowering his eyes, flicked it back over his shoulder to George Nicholson — who dropped it. 'First dropped ball on English soil,' said Jimmy Duncan. Poor George looked sorry about that. One of the reporters asked us if we could do *it* again and Jimmy said, 'No. We never make the same mistake twice.' It was amazing how quickly we found our voice and style, without thought so it seemed, like the wilfulness of water or the way light will bounce off in every direction at once.

Now a well-spoken man from the English Rugby Union welcomed the team to England and George Tyler, missing a front tooth, passed his hand across his mouth.

We breakfasted at the Duke of Cornwall, in a blue room the shape of the globe, bacon and eggs, tea and toast, then boarded the train to Newton Abbot.

two

making a
name for
ourselves

two

We had arrived to a tidy world
a spoken for world
We lined the carriage windows
and gaped at the thatched cottages
at the tidy figure in the paddock
the tame hedgerows
There appeared to be little in the way of landscaping left to do.
At the Globe in Newton Abbot we sat on the edge of our made beds.
Now what? we wondered.
Jimmy Duncan called a practice.
We felt oddly self-conscious.
We did not want to interrupt England.
We did not want to draw attention to ourselves.
We practised our scrum, our special 'wedge' formation devised off Tierra del Fuego.
Billy Stead got the backs going — Billy Wallace and Mona Thompson in from their wings, weaving inside and out, first Billy on the cut, then Mona. Freddy Roberts on a drifting run, the inside pass to Jimmy Hunter who links with Smithy. In this way we began to sow our patterns onto the lovely English field.
Our first injury on English soil: McDonald tore an ear at practice.

For some days the ocean foamed in our ears. The Atlantic continued to roll beneath the English streets. In the lobby of the Globe Hotel, Frank Glasgow threw his arms around a column. Billy Wallace steadied himself as if catching his balance on an unsteady log. The English hotel maids giggled behind their hands as Billy Stead's arms flew up and he yelled 'whoaaah!' on a run across the sloping red carpet to the safety of the bar rail.

We woke to English sounds — the scullery, slushing water, roosters, crows, the shuffle of tea trolleys, the song of the washerwoman squeezing her mop at the end of the hall. We lay in our beds, cataloguing these scraps of 'Englishness' for future use. Later we sat up in our beds and pulled back a corner of the curtain to see what was happening down in the street. We could see donkeys with kindling tied to their flanks wobbling down the hill lanes to the market outside the hotel, where thick-ankled women in white pilgrim shawls set down vegetable baskets next to the loaves and round cheeses. In the first few days we were like shy crayfish. We weren't sure how to place ourselves in that scene outside our window. On the first morning we watched Billy Glenn then Corbett try to insert themselves — Billy Glenn with his hands behind his back and the false calm of someone determined to ignore a growling dog; we saw him lean forward then it was as if his feet wouldn't carry him any further. Corbett took a more direct route to the bread cart; once there, he looked fiercely up and down the main street. Then a local happened to ask him a question and Bill took a backward step, fright took hold of his face, he shook his head and hurried away back to the hotel lobby. Jimmy Duncan wandered at leisure to a park bench by the watch tower. He yawned into his hand and plopped himself down, crossed his legs and lay his head back to bathe in the early morning sunshine. It was a lesson to us all.

We took heart from Jimmy's lead and soon were a familiar sight about Newton Abbot. We were invited out to musicals and theatres, to public smoking concerts. At the invitation of Lord Clifford and the Earl of Devon, Gallaher, Jimmy Duncan, Billy Stead and Mister Dixon went for a ride in a motor car and came swaggering back to the Globe with shining faces. They'd travelled over one hundred miles into the English countryside. The rest of us walked. Or we cycled. We cycled through the green countryside to Teignmouth, Totes, Paington. Along the Devonshire lanes we saw elements of 'time' and 'order' bundled up in thick hedgerows, backed by wide-spreading elms, fern, ivy, mosses and wild flowers. And when you looked at those elms and mosses and wild flowers you found yourself looking past them to the gorsey clay hillsides of home. In one you saw the start of something and in the other the pretty finish.

Did we feel at home? Among the English, and English things?
But we had these things too: sparrows, thrushes, macrocarpas. Tea and potatoes.
On the coast walk between Carbis Bay and St Ives, we found the odd patch of gorse, even cabbage trees.
We recognised the mould from which we'd been cast. In the mannerisms and transactions of the people, we saw ourselves —
the way a barman with one neat action sweeps the bar top dry before setting down a pint of Guinness
the chirpy skill of the fruiterer filling the bag with apples and spinning it to a twist at the opening
the matey banter of the cabbies, and the tenderness with which they spoke to their horses: 'Go on 'ome with yer Samantha'
the knowledge of oceans contained in the faces of the Devon and Cornishmen
the same measuring sideways glance out the corner of an Irishman's face when a leg-pull was on
and this! the same nutty obsession for the state of the weather
and that English silence aboard trains, wily as trout
the choreography and fair play of the English in numbers; first, the women and the children, then the gentlemen
the time given to the discussion of dogs
or, on the stillest of mornings, with the world hanging by a thread,

the maniacal urge to laugh at the top of our voices

That was us as well.

Time and time again, we'd catch them looking at us,
measuring and evaluating.
They felt our biceps
asked us to step up on the scales
stared down our throats
counted our teeth
and challenged us to Indian arm wrestles.

Then that first game in Devon
Played in golden farmlight.

On the train up to Exeter we hardly spoke to one another.
Our attention wandered out the carriage window but nothing caught our interest.
A sail boat.
An elderly couple, the man with only one arm holding a fishing rod.
A dog wagged its tail.
The world didn't look a serious enough place for our mood.
Where the train left the coast to follow the edge of a marshland Mister Dixon got to his feet; he scratched himself and looked perplexed. He walked up and down a few times. He fossicked in his pocket for his speech notes and tips on VIP greetings.

In Exeter we visited the great cathedral and walked around the city streets. We were supposedly taking an interest but O'Sullivan and Stead kept needing to find a toilet, and Mister Dixon kept disappearing into the graveyard with his speech notes.

After lunch at the Half Moon Hotel, our two coaches followed the river to the County Ground. We crossed the river, passed under a bridge and turned down a narrow street of houses. At the end of the street we could see long lines of people passing through the gates, the men in caps and top hats and the women in sun bonnets. We sunk back in our seats, eyes averted to the coach upholstery.

Christ! They were coming to see us! We closed our eyes and silently prayed that we wouldn't make fools of ourselves.

Entering the ground we tried not to look but couldn't help ourselves. In every direction you saw people. The stand was full, and the area behind the bike track; between there and the rows of houses people stood five, six, seven deep while up on the roofline solitary figures clung to chimney pots.

At 3 pm we walk out in single file, Glasgow pulling his headgear on. O'Sullivan trips on a clod of mud and reddens with embarrassment. Billy Wallace's eyes dart to all corners of the field; he locates the posts, takes a couple of backward steps then jogs back. Billy Stead notes the roll of the turf and where at one corner it slopes away on the grandstand side of the ground. Gallaher bends down to pick up a clod of mud and throws it away. Steve Casey underarms a pebble. Jimmy Hunter wipes away a nervous yawn. In the short time that it takes us to walk out to the middle we look for a dozen diversions.

Then a crow flew across the ground and every one of us looked up to follow its flight. Our eyes swam in the blue skies. The sunny day was nothing like what we'd been told to expect at this time of year. George Gillett wore a tweed hat at fullback.

Our first points on English soil came within three minutes of the start. Fred clears from a scrum to Billy Stead, a sweet transfer to Jimmy Hunter. Jimmy runs hard at the defensive line; the Devon men try to wrap him up but Jimmy's legs keep pumping and that's when we first saw the alarm on the faces of the Devon players. You saw the Devon men back on their heels, hands in the air. Jimmy was supposed to fall over. Every other player they wrapped up falls over. They weren't used to Jimmy's civil disobedience. But a horse wouldn't have stopped Jimmy. Behind his maddening release of energy were six weeks at sea, hours of shipboard training, hours spent imagining such a moment as this, through ice storms and tropical heat. Jimmy spins free, as easy as passing through a revolving door and goes over near the posts for Billy Wallace to convert. That was just the beginning. George Smith crossed for four tries. Carbine got three. George Gillett went over for a try with one hand holding on to the brim of his sun hat. We scored twelve tries in all and were up by fifty points before Devon answered with a penalty goal.

The ease with which we did it surprised everyone, the crowd, the newspapermen, ourselves included. We heard later that several London newspapers came out the following day with the wrong score. The telegraph operator transcribing the dots to letters had 'corrected' the 55–4 scoreline to read in favour of the English County champions.

Later that afternoon in the chandeliered light of a hotel in Exeter we rose with the Devon men to toast the King and sing our national anthems. We were so happy and with the champagne glowing in our cheeks we belted out a haka that had the ashtrays and champagne flutes bouncing on the tabletops.

Outside the hotel a huge cheer went up. Thousands stood in the dark where earlier in the day we'd passed unnoticed. They wanted to shake our hands. They slapped our backs. They seemed to know us or want to know us. We shook their hands. 'God bless,' they said. God bless. We smiled with uncertainty, wondering if this was the right thing to do.

They were so appreciative and we were so grateful.

◆

News of what had happened at the County Ground had reached

Newton Abbot around six that evening. The stationmaster was first to hear. He'd tipped his cap and shaken hands with Jimmy Duncan earlier in the day. He wrote down the score on a scrap of paper and sent one of his assistants off with it to the innkeeper. Within a short time the news had passed along the doors, from house to house. Now it was just after eleven at night, and as we stepped from the train a huge crowd of men, women, children and their dogs cheered as we made our way to the drays to take us to the hotel. A brass band walked ahead of us through the main street of town playing 'The Road to Moscow'. As we arrived at the Globe the hotel manager raced out in his shirtsleeves to greet us. We climbed down from the dray and the excited crowd closed in around us. They wouldn't let us inside until they'd heard some words. Say something to us. Speak! So, from the upstairs balcony, Mister Dixon leant his weight on the balustrade as we'd seen him do so often at the ship rail and put across a typically modest view. 'Naturally we believe in our system, but it would be premature, premature I think, on the strength of one match to express an opinion about it . . .' The crowd looked disappointed. The voice didn't quite match the deed. The content wasn't quite there. They shuffled restlessly. George Nicholson correctly read their mood and with Cunningham rallied us for a haka. '. . . who! who! ra! ra!' They loved that; they clapped and begged for more. They pulled on our shoulders and who-raaaed in our faces. They wanted to hear more. Mister Dixon looked at his timepiece. Nicholson, though, slapped his long thighs and Cunningham rolled his eyes. Pakeha atea! Ring a ring a pakeha . . . The street thrilled. The dogs howled in the English night.

◆

'The first impression of the New Zealanders was interesting. Their whole costume is black. Black jersey with a silver fern leaf, black knickers, black stockings and boots. One funny item was that the whole team came out in pink elastic knee bandages and anklets which had a very peculiar effect . . .'

'Their skins are of an equable brownish olive tint . . .'

'Their kit is, to begin with, jet black, and that must strike their opponents rather forcibly at the outset. Then each jersey has a sort of deeper yoke of a different material, the yoke of the jersey worn by the three-quarters, the five-eighths, and halfback, is made of silk, and is therefore slippery to touch as is compatible with safety . . .'

'They work together like the parts of a well-constructed watch. Wherever a man is wanted, there he is!'

'They had the true athlete's walk, shoulders above the hips . . .'

'There is a note of what might be called desperation — or, better still, desperateness in the play of the New Zealanders . . . Somebody said of Lord Beaconsfield as a debater, "He talks like a horse racing — he talks all over." That is how the New Zealanders play, as if their hope of eternal welfare depends upon success. Every nerve and sinew braced all but to snapping point.'

'There is a complete absence of all that noise with which habitués of London Football grounds are only too well acquainted.'

'Our side were like a lot of cowboys, compared to them.' Mr Carter, ex-President of the Devon Rugby Football Club

'One could not help being struck with the magnificent physique of the team, Cunningham, the forward, known as the "lock" or centre scrummager of the second rank, being especially a splendid example of humanity.'

❖

We began to feel better about ourselves.

❖

We attracted a record gate for our second game against Cornwall.
Again it was the same story —
Nicholson forced over from a loosies' rush
Abbott was next on the end of a long pass from Roberts. Seeling too,
then Smith in transit — bumped through — Wallace converted —
Deans got over after the passing went Roberts, Mynott, Hunter, Smith,
Deans.
Roberts, Mynott, Hunter worked the blind side successfully — Wallace
converting — Hunter dodged through for the try,
Wallace the conversion.

We began to float and to achieve a kind of grace that had become
second nature, like language or riding a bike.

One night Frank Glasgow sat down at the piano and composed music
to describe the English style of play; it went — plonk plonk plonk plonk,
plonk.
You heard that and saw the English shift the ball across field, one two
three four stop and kick for touch.
To describe our play Frank came up with this number — dum de dah
dum de dah bang whoosh bang! whoosh dum de dah clicketty-click
bang! whoosh dah
or Roberts to Stead on the loop around Hunter, on to Smith bursting
clear or finding support in Thompson, Booth, or Wallace wide
or, as the defence gathers around Hunter
the skip pass from Stead to Smith — Gallaher, Casey, O'Sullivan in
support
ball to ground, cleared by Fred to Mona/Carbine/Bunny racing down
the touch line.

It was music new to English ears:
they weren't used to the fullback chiming in outside the wing to score
tries
they weren't used to the ball travelling through so many hands
they weren't used to the forwards mingling with the backs

the form unsettled them, they said

they weren't used to our scrum formation — its two-man front row 'specialist positions', they said, were new to them

the wing forward position presented a philosophical problem: was Gallaher a back or a forward? They rolled their bottom lip beneath their teeth. They were unsure as to his entitlements.

Through the rest of September and October into November it was the same thing. Cornwall, Bristol, Northampton, Leicester, Middlesex, Durham, Hartlepool, Northumberland, Gloucester — they stuck to what they knew, which is what they had been brought up with, and we got into the habit of saying, 'You'd think they'd have learnt by now.' We quite liked saying that, and therefore said it as often as we could — 'You'd think they'd have learned something by now . . .' It must have got on Mister Dixon's nerves because at Taunton one evening, at 'debates', he instructed us on the ways of compassion.

What, he asked, do you say to the man who, running late for his wedding, has never seen or heard of a motorcar?

To the single-string bush banjo player who weeps over his simple twanging instrument but who has never heard a cello?

How do you describe a sunset to the blind?

What is appealing about new possibilities for those who don't seek them?

Unusually for Mister Dixon, whose complexion ran to a sandy ginger, some colour entered his cheeks. 'About the blind,' he said. 'I just threw that in as an example.'

Gallaher removed his pipe and cast an eye over the room to invite submissions.

Simon Mynott cleared his throat. He sat up straight and raked his fingers back through his thinning hair. 'Louise Farrow,' he said. 'Now Louise is a case in point. Gorgeous. She has this honey-coloured hair that darkens in winter and . . . well . . . her husband drowned when she was just twenty-three. She put up his photograph in every room. Frank. Frank Pritchard. That was his name. The poor drowned bastard. Anyway. Frank this, Frank that. Frankly,' he said — and he looked around to see if we had got that. ('Still here, Simon,' said Jimmy Duncan.) 'Anyway,' said Simon, 'you never got anything else out of her. Not a peep. This good-looking, gorgeous woman. But she was stuck with her husband. Stuck with his death. She wore black. Every man who came to her house remained the plumber or the painter, or the coal man, or the postie or the bloke selling eggs. Never a bloke bloke, if you know what I mean.'

'Thank you, Simon,' said Mister Dixon.
'Possibilities,' someone else said, 'is knowing how to recognise them.'
This seemed wise, if in an imprecise way, and those with pipes struck attitudes of thought.

◆

At Camborne against the Cornwall men we started against the hill and the sun. The only elements in our way, as it turned out. A local pen-and-pad man wrote: 'They walked right through us as if we were a sheet of paper.'
We racked up 41 points, and a few days later put up the same score against Bristol.

After Camborne the pad-and-pencil men never left our side. They stood in our shadows, them and their long gazes. They wanted to interview us but we didn't do interviews. We did our talking on the field. The morning after a match saw us clambering down various stairways to get to the newspapers to see what they had to say —
we were 'slippery as eels'
'persistent as wasps'
'clever and alert as monkeys'
'[we] worked together like the parts of a well-constructed watch'

making a name for ourselves

we were 'Trojans of the scrum'
'backs of modern Mercury'
at Limerick we were 'Maori Marvels'
'full of originality and resource'
'wizards'
'human will o' the wisp'
we showed 'sleuth-hound persistency' against Glamorgan
against Oxford we were 'razor-edged'
'bewildering'
'loose-limbed'
'consummate showmen' at Hollow Drift against the Bedford fifteen
'powerful'
'dazzling — the ball switching hands 14 times before McGregor
waltzed over'
against Munster we were 'conjurors of magic'

'Roberts dived for the line. Like a panther, Maclear was on him and
pinned him to the ground. They went over Catherine wheel style. Lo
and behold, when we looked again Abbott was resting the ball for a
try. How did he get it? Where did it come from? Didn't it look like magic?'

After we beat Northampton 32–nil the *Telegraph* man wrote: 'The
situation is becoming quite alarming.'

Following the Northampton match the townfolk cheered us all the
way back to the Plough Hotel; that night the music halls and theatres
were thrown open to us.
A record gate turned up to see us play Leicester and on our way to
Franklin Gardens the men waved to us in our brakes and women
fluttered their kerchiefs along the route. It was a huge crowd, and when
we walked out a whisper circled the ground — 'Where is he? Which

one is he?' Gallaher had been singled out for his wing forward play; certain newspaper critics bristled at his neither-here-nor-there position. They didn't like his roving commission. Was he a forward or was he a back? He fed the scrum, threw in to the lineout, stalked the opposing halves, disrupted their ball, and led the dribbling rushes. When we took the field Dave let their stares roll off him; he stood on one leg and picked the mud from the cleats of his boots.

We beat Leicester 28–nil and the pad-and-pencil men wrote: 'We have been made, in the noble Cromwellian phrase, like stubble before swords.' '. . . Mynott thread his way through opponents like an eel, while Smith jumped over our men just as if he was in a hurdle race . . .' Billy Wallace was described as a 'cross between a greyhound and a flash of lightning'.

After Middlesex (34–nil) we were compared to blood horses, 'while the gait of the Middlesex men is more suggestive of the tramp of the shire Stallion'.

On to Durham, another record gate, and in the long wet grass at Hollow Drift we stuttered to 16–3 in drizzly rain. Mynott had a cold. Casey a bruised shoulder. Dunk McGregor's knee was troubling him. McDonald's arm was in a sling.

At Hartlepool the police stopped the sale of tickets half an hour before the game which we went on to win 63–nil. Seven times we scored in succession; the only time the Hartlepool men touched the ball was to kick off. The local newspaperman wrote: 'It was bewildering and the crowd stood as one man, entranced . . .'

Jimmy Hunter picked up five tries against Northumberland (31–nil). 'Their adaptability is really their greatest virtue. The man who was fullback at Leicester was wing forward at North Shields.'

For the match against Gloucester we were met at the railway station by a huge crowd which walked behind our drays all the way to the hotel, 'a following you'd see at a circus arriving in town'. After the game, a pad-and-pencil man quoted a spectator: 'What went ye to see? A weed shaken by the wind?'

These were good words to start the day with. When you left the hotel you felt a lift in the soles of your feet. The air seemed to be waiting for you to breathe it. The gruff little bugger at the fruit barrow threw in an extra apple.

❖

Our eleventh game brought us to Taunton. The streets were postered with 'Come and see the wonderful All Blacks.'

'When the Somerset men arrived on the field there was an encouraging cheer, but the Colonials, although enthusiastically welcomed, were gazed at with such curiosity that the crowd almost forgot to welcome them.'

By now, we'd moved from the world of ordinary men.

We were the stuff of the shop window
What children's birthdays are made of
We were Christmas
The bubble in the pop
The jam on the bread
We were the place smiles come from

Wherever we went we were accompanied by a stage and a small brass band.
'Ladies and gentlemen, I give you . . .'

We understood the interest. We knew what it was like to stand at a ship rail and without warning or expectation to have a shoal of brilliantly coloured flying fish turn your head.

Our 'equable brownish olive tints'
offered proof of 'the new way of life'
advertised in the *Somerset County Gazette*.

Taunton's hotels and eating houses struggled to cope with the invasion. Long lines formed outside restaurant doors, and that night the out-of-town spectators slept in the extra hundred cars laid on by the railways for the purpose.

As early as one o'clock the Jarvis Field began to fill; by 2.30 no one could move. One of the makeshift stands collapsed but no one was hurt or especially bothered. That section of crowd simply resettled itself in the manner of birds shaken out of a tree. When we ran out to defend the 'station goal' the crowd's stare lengthened and intensified and we realised they were 'window-shopping'.

We were embarrassed by our efforts. But 20 of our party were suffering from various injuries and illness. Boils. Poisoned legs. We set about rejigging the backline. We rested Hunter and Roberts. Stead went to halfback; Mynott and Deans served in the five-eighths department. It was not a success. Several times tries went begging for our failure to shift the ball wide. Nicholson knocked on with the line before him. On another occasion O'Sullivan's pass was ruled forward, and so it went, our enterprise seemingly directed into ways of sabotaging our skill. The field, we realised, was too narrow. The space we usually basked in just wasn't there. We still ran out winners 23 to nil. But for the first time we found ourselves complaining and reaching for excuses, and for the first time, as well, we heard the pad-and-pencil men scratch on their paper and begin to mutter: 'Wait till they get to Wales . . .'

At Plymouth we played Albion (21–3). A stand was given up to invalids from the nearby military hospital. In glorious sunshine, the Mayor kicked off and dashed back to his place in the stand.

For the match against Midland Counties (21–5) the Midlands Railway Workers were given half a day off on full pay to watch us play.

After Surrey (11–nil) the pad-and-pencil men turned on the 'whistling ref'.

At Blackheath (32–nil) we were described as artists and creatures of the stage. 'To watch the "Hamlet"-clad lot retrieve a failure is almost as interesting as the excitement at their customary swooping or rush of attack . . . There is always somebody under-studying for the time-being, the player is hors de combat. Into the breach the new "artist" without a second's hesitation goes.'

Oxford (47–nil): we remember Hunter's doggy grin as he jogged back from another try and the joke in the newspaper. 'One undergraduate to an older one: "Why don't our men tackle 'em?" Replies the other: "My son, if you read the rules you would know you are not allowed to tackle a man until you have caught him."'

Cambridge (14–nil) were made of sturdier stuff.

Richmond (17–nil). The rain fell in torrents and all around the ground rang the sour cries of 'Gallaher play the game.'

❖

By November 16 we had amassed 626 points for, to 15 against.

❖

Then we played four matches in eight days.

Bedford (41–nil) we remember for the hailstorm minutes before kickoff and their recruiting outside players, notably the giant Irish international, Maclear. We paid him an early visit: 'His Blackhealth stockings showing above the Blacks' heads.'

Scotland (12–7) was a narrow escape. The Scots were the first side to score first against us.

West of Scotland we beat (22–nil) on a soft turf.

Ireland (15–nil): during a break in play when officials searched to replace a burst ball we chatted with the Irish. Billy Wallace's opposite asked him if he was interested in motor cars.

Munster (33–nil) was Bill Mackrell's first game on tour. We lost George Smith to broken ribs.

England (15–nil). Dunk McGregor's four tries stand out, that and the premier stand filled with dukes, earls and other notables.

We put on another 52 points against Cheltenham and Cheshire.

Yorkshire (40–nil). We arrived at the ground in motor cars. The old members of the Yorkshire men who'd played the Natives in 1888 sat together in specially reserved seats.

Wales 0–3. We lost. We what . . .? More on that later.

Between December 16 and 30 a crushing itinerary asked us to play five matches. By then we were reduced to fielding whoever was fit enough to play.

Glamorgan 9–nil.

Newport 6–3.

Cardiff 10–8.

Against Swansea, who'd just lost to Cardiff for the first time in three years, we scraped by 4–3.

◆

In the silky pages of *The Times* we found ourselves mentioned alongside foreign countries, statesmen and other notables. Bristol was the first occasion. The match account was short but still longer than a report on the bomb explosion at Peking Railway Station.

versus Northampton, 32–nil. *The Times* gave us 24 lines, six lines more than report on 'New Anglo-Japanese Treaty' and 18 lines more than a brief piece on the 'Morocco Question'.

versus Leicester — 35 lines! Still disappointing . . . eight lines less than a report on 'abnormal tides' and details of Lieutenant Colonel Theophilus Vaughton Dymock's estate. On the other hand, the match report was still longer than articles on 'Italian Earthquakes', a proposed 'Austro-Chinese Bank', and a report on 'Congress on Tuberculosis'.

The Times' description of Smithy: '. . . nothing was so remarkable as the way in which G.W. Smith, the centre three-quarter, took the ball at top speed; and continually swept through opponents . . .' is twice as long as a report on 'Australian Revenue Returns', and this grisly report out of Southern Russia: 'The mob placed a number of Jews in barrels and trundled them along until they were dead . . . A large cage filled with Jews was thrown into the river . . .'

versus Middlesex at Stamford Bridge — 45 lines! though, this is 85 lines less than the excessively long report on the 'National Chrysanthemum Society's Show'. Looking at it more closely the match description turns out to be longer than the discussion of 'chrysanthemum's origins'. Gallaher also points out that praise of our tackling is not only lengthier but in prose more rapturous than the descriptive account of the 'early flowering Japanese varieties'.

versus Durham — a miserly 38 lines in *The Times*.

versus Hartlepool — 35 lines, which is eight lines less than 'the kennel club show at Crystal Palace'.
Terribly disappointing, and yet . . . the boys earned 31 lines more than 'the German Steamer captured by Japanese', 19 lines more than the betrothal of Prince Friedrich of Prussia' and 'Chinese Outrages in Johannesburg'.

versus Northumberland, back on track. 52 lines in *The Times*, 27 lines more than 'bomb outrages in Warsaw'.

versus Devonport Albion — 50 lines, 40 lines more than that given to 'Mr Roosevelt on Lynch Laws'.

versus Midland Counties — 72 lines! in *The Times* . . . plus 92 lines on 'The Revolution in Rugby Football'.
More than 'bloodshed in Odessa', 'Russian Warship Mutiny', 'The Conflict in Hungary' and 'Lord Rosebery's address on Scottish history' combined.

versus Surrey — 51 lines. Lost ground to 'rioting in Warsaw' and

'Strikes in Finland', plus 'Scarcity of meat in Germany'.

versus Cambridge — 95 lines!

versus Richmond — 67 lines.

The Times notes thus far, 571 points racked up in 18 victories, no defeats, conceding 15 points.

versus Bedford — 55 lines. Plague in India — 13 lines.

versus Scotland — 160 lines!

versus Ireland — 140 lines!

versus Munster — 38 lines: rain.

versus England — 170 lines!!! Only the obituaries longer.

versus Cheshire — 40 lines, two lines more than death of 'Mr Humphreys-Owen, MP' and twice as long as the report on *Salome*, the new Richard Strauss opera staged in Dresden. 'The composer, who conducted, was called before the curtain 40 times . . .' We didn't even play that well. Everywhere there are signs of fatigue and Stead has boils.

versus Wales — 150 lines in *The Times* we could do without.
The story begins two-thirds down the column and the eye is distracted by two advertisements opposite: one for 'Peterkin: the story of a dog' and the other for Enos Fruit Salts 'to remove morning gloom'.

making a name for ourselves

three

fame's arrow

three

There are other moments that need to be acknowledged, spoken of,
catalogued. Moments that simply occupy time between conquests.

The walk along the chalk cliffs
the snare of history
in the whitish air
No one talking, and
because of it
quite naturally our thoughts
turning to
Vikings.

Or at Scarborough, the striped deckchairs
the ferris wheel
the buttoned-up English
Tyler's throwing a dart
and winning a stuffed rabbit
and us throwing it around a bit
until Jimmy Duncan scratched his chin
and thought he'd mention
an error he'd seen creep into our play.

The ride out to North Cliffs

O'Sullivan, Casey, McDonald
leaning into the Atlantic wind
hands in pockets
wondering
but not really finding anything, and so
drifting into private space
until Jimmy Duncan gave the word
'Pack it in, shall we?'

The tours of factories
where we watched other men at work
and stuffed our pockets with pipes, cigarettes
& bicycle parts.

Visits to cathedrals, abbeys, ruins,
to old prisons,
Invitations to dine, to plays, dramas, music halls,
to shop
and search out
relatives.

Blackpool. Seagulls. Predators with black teeth
stolen goods in their rotten pockets.

Booth winning a box of chocolates at the coconut shy.

Glasgow swinging a hammer to send a red flag to the top of the pole
and breaking all records.

We placed two five-men teams in the swimming relays and beat the
Hornsey Swimming Club champions.

We could thrash Middlesex in the afternoon 34–nil and out-swim the
Woodsiders in the evening at the South Norwood Pool.

England felt like a place specially created
for us to excel.

❖

In London, fame was measurable.
You could walk around it
Look it in the eye
and admire it.

At Madame Tussaud's we tiptoed around the Shah of Persia, Garibaldi, Shakespeare. Interesting to see which famous figure drew who: Seeling squaring off before the pugilist William Cobbett, Nicholson leaning forward to inspect Doctor Livingstone, George Smith winking at PT Barnum, Jimmy Duncan folding his arms before Lord Nelson, the back-heeled lean of Billy Stead and Billy Wallace inquiring of Sir Richard Burton of the desert. The rest were mainly military types, a clutch of church leaders and royalty. Mister Dixon took a solemn interest in the execution of Mary, Queen of the Scots.

Outside Tussaud's, we noticed that unless you were a Lord or Viscount or Admiral you worked hard to get your name in the newspaper. Something out of the ordinary pitched your name forward. For example, the woman who spent fifty-one years in bed after a mistaken diagnosis; or a much younger woman who died of apoplexy from laughter at a pantomine.

'Shooting himself with a revolver, Baron Salomon de Gunsborg, formerly a banker, committed suicide in Paris, yesterday.'

'Miss Morris, a teacher in high school in Chesterfield, Iowa, was lecturing on electricity when she was struck by lightning . . .'

'The yacht *Catarina*, in which the absconding French bank clerk Galley sailed to South America, is due at Gospert in about a week's time.'

So we were surprised when we found ourselves
in the *Illustrated London News,*
sharing the limelight
with the Russian uprising,
portraits of Tolstoy,
the auctioning of Napoleon's chair,
and a series of illustrations
demonstrating the Indian method
of using elephants
to crush offenders to death.

◆

From the Manchester Hotel we walked to the National Portrait Gallery in Trafalgar Square. There, we toured the gallery halls and gaped back at the famous faces which seemed to want us to know them. Explorers, engineers, architects.

Under a portrait of Augustus Welby Northmore Pugin young Steve Casey found himself baled up by a finger-pointing autodidact.

'You have to wonder, Why this person and not that one. I mean, have you ever thought about this. No one to my knowledge has ever painted or drawn a rat, artistically, I mean, as far as I know. There are no famous rat paintings. Name me one now and I'll eat my hat. There are famous horse paintings. Christ, you could fill a ship's hold with those. Grouse. One or two of them get on to the canvas. Even a bloody farm hen. You know the sort of thing. Wolves. Foxes. Cats. Dogs, and that's all right with dogs, I suppose. But then it gets ridiculous with parrots, pheasants, quail, fish — often as not on serving platters but nonetheless represented. Snakes. Elephants. Giraffes. Your elephant lumbers in at this point. Whales bursting up around men with harpoons in open boats. Only your rat is overlooked.

'But I'm bashing your ear, son. What is it you do?'

Casey caught us up and we passed into another hall, this one displaying 'famous groups' —

'The 7 Bishops Committed to the Tower in 1688'
'The Gun Powder Plot Conspirators'
'The Five Children of Charles 1'
'Men of Science Living in 1807–8'
'Swinburne and his Sisters'
'The Anti-Slavery Convention, 1840'
'Four men at Cards'
and so on . . . but none like us. At the end of the hall Gallaher and
Stead looked at each other, and it was an even race as to who got it out
first: 'No football teams.'

Put up that year were —
Cecil Rhodes
'the religious fanatic and impostor' Joanna Southcott
the poets Thomas Campbell and Thomas Love Peacock
the Rajah of Sarawak
Sir Rowland Hill, 'initiator of penny post'
Toberius Cavallo, author of *A Complete Treatise on Electricity*,
& Captain James Cook

We found ourselves admired
Lord Mayors felt our biceps
Luminaries of the theatre world invited us backstage

A famous acrobat from the 1870s performed a handstand on a dinner
chair at Bunny Abbott's request
An 'associate' of the man who invented steam said to Eric Harper, 'If
there's anything I can do . . .'
A military man who owned tea plantations in India travelled 35 miles
to challenge George Tyler to an arm wrestle

They passed on notes of introduction
Shook our hands
said 'what an honour it is . . .'

The hand this or that Mayor shook was as often as not a hand that held a plough
or shovel or teat
Didn't seem to matter though
At half-time against Gloucester the Duke of Northumberland came down for a chat
and invited us to inspect his castle

Mister Dixon warned us of 'trophy hunters'. 'Tehiddy.' He looked around for Dave Gallaher. 'Remember, Dave?' It was the day before we thrashed Cornwall and the local tin magnate invited the two of them to his estate. 'I've never seen a private library like it. First editions. Bibles in ancient Greek and Hebrew. Some clay tablets picked up from a Somalian grave. Lion skins on the wall. Zebra skins covering the floor. Port from a bottle corked in seventeen hundred and something.' He paused here to relight his pipe, and when it was burning grunted, 'Do you know the Bassetts employ a fulltime cricketer just to have around?'

'You met him?' asked Massa.

'No, son. I'm standing in the library with Bassett admiring his antiques when I happen to glance up and out the window and see this fellow in white flannels standing on the lawn next to the Etruscan fountain. So to Mr Bassett I say, "Who's that gentleman I see?" And he says, "Him? Why that's my Australian cricketer, Bill Thorn. I have his stats somewhere."'

Mister Dixon pulled on the ends of his moustache and we fell about laughing, though he claims 'the cricketer part is true'.

People hung on to every
word said

Sometimes what we said
hell, it didn't even make sense
not that it seemed to matter
not to them
or us

'So, you've never eaten snails, Mr Gallaher?'
'No, but I'm planning to when I get to France.'
'Interesting.'
'And how do you find the food in the United Kingdom?'
'Can't complain.'
'So, no complaints?'
'No, not really . . . Except . . .'
'Yes? Go on . . .'
'Well I was going to say . . . But no, we've no complaints.'

◆

One morning we are visited by a small nervous man, a museum
curator, who asks if we can give him something. Jimmy Duncan thinks
he means money, but quickly withdraws his hand from his pocket
when the man adds, '. . . anything at all, really.'

McGregor and McDonald happen to be playing noughts and crosses
on a table napkin. Jokingly, McGregor holds up the napkin with the
game on it and asks if this will do, and the little man, the curator, well,
his face grows keen. He gives a small greedy nod, then he asks, 'I
wonder, would you boys mind signing it?'

The curator closes his hand over his mouth to stifle a yelp.

'Both signatures. Please,' he says, and bites his hand.

Jimmy Duncan laughs. 'Next you'll be wanting our train tickets.' The curator turns his head to look at Jimmy, and his lower lip drops. He bites his hand again, and nods. So Jimmy has to pull out his Leeds to Cardiff ticket. Jimmy Hunter fishes out a London to Oxford stub. Soon everyone is emptying their pockets and old theatre tickets and train tickets are falling to the carpet and the curator is scrambling on his knees to collect them all.

Bob Deans hands over a pair of cufflinks. Billy Glenn unknots his tie and gives him that. George Nicholson gives the man a handful of boot sprigs. It had started out as a joke but soon a small box has to be found. We fill this and a broken suitcase that we have no further use for, and hold the door for the curator to haul his booty off. When a gust of wind removes his hat we are surprised that he doesn't stop for it; and turning away from the door we look at one another, and it is about then that we realise we have been looted.

❖

In Dublin as Dave Gallaher stepped from the train a young newspaperman bounded up to him. 'Mr Gallaher. Mr Gallaher, sir. How does it feel to be famous?' Gallaher told him, 'The pyramids are famous, son.' We liked that; we liked Dave's gruff dose of wisdom. But there was little time for Dave to expand because then the barriers holding back the crowd fell apart and the Dubliners swarmed towards us.

Ireland knew about us. She had been expecting us. All the flags were out. We were received like royalty at the Dublin Guinness plant. We climbed aboard a miniature train and wound in and out the barrels of Guinness stacked on end like cotton reels.

At Petersen's Pipe Factory we got about like trade commissioners. Each of us was given a pipe. George Dixon held his under his nose. Steve Casey and Bill Mackrell stuck theirs in their pockets and looked around for the next treat.

That night the audience stood and cheered us as we filed into the

Empire Palace Theatre to take our seats.

The applause continued the next day as we wandered Dublin's streets. Men tipped their hats. Women smiled up beneath their hat brims. The wild shrieks belonged to small boys discovering us at the end of an alley or across the street. It was impossible to take in a statue with so many eyes on us. Dublin knew who we were, and every corner of the city appeared to have been expecting us the moment we showed up. We paused to regroup and the doors of a tavern flew open. A publican in a white apron appeared with a large tray of malt whiskies. It was the wrong time of day to be drinking but Mister Dixon gave his consent. The publican nodded encouragement and while we went about the malts a small boy scampered around our legs asking, 'Which one are yer, Billy Wallace?' Billy Stead pointed him out, and the boy dropped to his knees, got out a piece of chalk and traced the outline of Billy Wallace's feet on the Dublin street.

◆

By now we were used to seeing ourselves on postcards hawked about town. In a London theatre we'd even seen ourselves up on screen. We got out our tobacco as the curtains parted on a huge white square. The lights dimmed and one or two of us looked around. Jimmy Duncan and Mister Dixon, obviously, as they were in charge of our safety and well-being. Then a yellow beam passed overhead and landed against the screen — not with any force but with the same effortlessness as pulling aside bedroom curtains and light finding the interior wall. Some numbers flickered up there. Then we saw pictures of ourselves. Life-like pictures. Limbs moving. Mona raking his fingers back through his hair. We left our pipes in our hands and moved to the edge of our seats. It was the strangest thing to sit down there and look up and see ourselves as others did. We stared at these shadows of ourselves. These likenesses. Fred looked like Fred, Billy Wallace like Billy Wallace, Jimmy Hunter himself but only more so. We watched our shadows perform knowledgeable tricks; and when you thought about it you realised that the shadows had to know their owners in order to be so convincing

fame's arrow

on screen. Our shadows remembered their origins spectacularly well. Things, personal things, previously intimate to ourselves. Fred Newton scratching himself. Billy Stead holding the front of his shorts out from himself to look down, looking for what? Massa closing one nostril to blow snot out the other. Now it was up there for all to see. There was some initial discomfort, but this soon passed and pleasure set in. We began to think about our haircuts and what in our appearance could be improved. Once we were able to tear our eyes away from ourselves, we got on with studying the shape of our game. It came as a shock to see what a mess the lineouts were in. Up to now we had imagined we formed a straight line. Then Booth dropped a ball and we all laughed. Bloody hell, any one of us could have caught that from where we sat. Billy Wallace missed an easy goal. Gillett missed two. Someone booed — in jest. But as we sunk into ourselves, our private selves, we realised that we did mind, seeing how gettable the chances were, and yet up on screen we saw ourselves back on our side of halfway, our hands on hips, and that we hadn't minded the misses.

On the field we moved to the whirring breath of cameras

Men crouched under black hoods aimed their tripods at us
or, as it sometimes happened
you might look up from breakfast
with a mouthful of toast
to find a man with a white napkin draped over his wrist
staring back

Moments of intimacy
when they came
snuck up on you
in the bath, alone
gazing up at the tiled walls
and on each tile
the impression of a peacock on its own
until you realised

that someone with a sketchpad
must have observed the moment
to capture it with a paintbrush
in order to say
'Here is a peacock alone in its peacock world'

We learned to appreciate those things
which are utmost and confidently themselves
a lily flat on a pond
the pattern of wallpaper in an empty hotel room
the last tree in a paddock
the barefoot beggar dragging his grey blanket past the fires down by
the river

We grew tired of our own company. It was too small a world to confine
ourselves. We found ourselves craving news of other lives, and so we
parted to visit our favourite monuments.

Billy Glenn to Speakers' Corner
Deans to the Westminster Cathedral
O'Sullivan & a loose forward trio
to the Tower of London

George Nicholson to the Isle of Dogs to find the coal man who sold
sheets of his music

Mackrell, Harper, Wallace, Gallaher and Messrs Duncan & Dixon to
the National Portrait Gallery

Billy Stead to the Euston Railway Station's public dictation room, from
where he brought back story after story

Stories of terrible loss, and in some cases grief or foolishness. Russian émigrés with frayed collars and still dressed in clothes from a fancy dress ball a month earlier. American heiresses with travel arrangements to send on to distant ports. Pompous voices, others that were urgent and charged with slight. 'We wish to inform you, sirs . . .' Penniless Italian Counts who would offload their sorry tale to Billy and try to hit him up for a florin while waiting for a stenographer to come free. Gamblers. Polish aristocrats who stood in line with heavy eyelids. There were the show-offs — lowly attention-seeking clerks Billy got to recognise and avoided like the plague. They'd borrow a white silk scarf from their employer to dictate in a plummy voice the terms of a make-believe will: '. . . and lastly, to my man Poutney, my horses and hunting dogs . . .' Others . . . sad, dishonoured men with maps of broken blood vessels tracking their cheeks dictated letters of sombre resignation to expensive and select clubs — 'Perhaps put in "no regrets". What do you think?' The stenographers were older women who kept a prim and discreet distance. The most they might allow themselves was a clipped, 'As you wish,' before their bony fingers raced back over the typewriter keys. There were letters from City gentlemen with their inside leg measurements to Indian tailors in Madras. The stenographers never flinched or showed so much as a sign that they had taken in this private information. They didn't appear interested in unscrambling the mysteries of other people's lives. So a man's inside leg measurement was taken down with the same detachment as they attended to the Putney birdwatcher's weekly correspondence with another in Aberdeen: 'Counted one hundred and twenty-nine black-birds on a guttering near Clapham Common at six twenty pm.' A South London butcher used coarse language in a threatening letter to an Oxford student of Romance languages warning him to stay away from his 'girl, Peg'. A young woman wrote to her admirer in Cologne. She had received his poem couriered by pigeon, thank you. It was indeed touching and beautiful . . . unfortunately she was replying with bad news. She wished to apologise from the bottom of her heart for the poisoned bread left out on the windowsill . . . A spoilt young wastrel in a party hat and reeking of brandy pushed past Billy to the head of the line. Swaying on his thin legs he shouted out the instruction that this was his last letter to his family, that in the future they would find his 'communications' written in condensation over the window of a Pall Mall tobacconist.

One afternoon Billy is waiting in line. As usual there are the familiar faces. A young fop with his inner leg measurement. An aggrieved Slav dictating a letter to the editor of *The Times*. A club man with his white shirt hanging out the back of his trousers has just finished dictating an apology to the host of a party. 'The glasses I can replace and Roger, please won't you convey my heartfelt apologies to Gwyneth. God knows what came over me . . .' As the stenographer calls 'next!' a slight commotion breaks out across the other side of the room. Someone has jumped the queue — a young man with dark rings around his eyes who holds his place and extends a hand behind him as if to keep the complaints at bay. He's in a white suit that is covered in grime and creases. He stands like someone hard of hearing, his chin tucked into his chest, eyes closed. When he speaks it is with difficulty as if the view he is reporting keeps shifting in and out of focus. As Billy watches the man presses his fingers to the sides of his head and begins with one word. Odessa. Something about the man's voice catches the attention of the other stenographers. It is rare for them to do so but one by one they turn their heads while their own clients continue to pick their thoughts from the air. Billy finds himself shifting closer in order to better hear —

Six hundred families homeless

Stop

Some of the ruffians put their victims to death by hammering nails in their heads

Stop

Eyes gouged out, ears cut off, tongues wrenched out with pincers

Stop

Number of women disembowelled

Stop

The aged and sick found huddling in cellars were soaked in petroleum and burnt alive

Stop

[64]

More to follow in the am
Stop

There was a silence — the only time Billy recalled one in the public
dictation room. The stenographer finished and dropped her hands to
her sides. From across the room another stenographer started up but
she too quickly realised her error and a few seconds later that
typewriter was silent as well.

There was silence as well in the lounge of the Manchester Hotel as
Billy reached the end of his account. Dave Gallaher awoke from his
slumber. He removed his heavy arms from the back of the couch. It
turned out he'd been listening after all. 'All right. All right. Let me ask
you all something. In a week's time it will be Sunday at home.
Overnight someone's favourite grandmother will have died. A young
boy, tragically, has drowned while crossing a flooded creek. A small
girl places her hands over her ears while the old man goes outside to
put a bullet through her lame horse "Rosalind". I could go on . . . But
I'm happy to stack those examples up on one side of the ledger, and,
the result of the match against Scotland on the other. Which one do
you think the people at home will want to hear and read about the
most?' Dave had us there but he wasn't finished. Encouraged by our
thoughtful silence he bounced up off the couch. 'Nope, wait. I've
changed my mind. This is better. Let's wipe those examples and put in
Billy's news from Russia about the slaughtering and so forth. Stack
that one up against our result and given the choice which one do you
think the people at home will want to hear? Which piece of news would
they give up to hear the other?'

You could have heard a pin drop.

'Exactly,' said Dave.

One more word on this subject.

THE BOOK OF FAME

That night Alec McDonald hears Mister Dixon with an English official in the foyer discussing Russia and the sinking of its Imperial fleet in the Sea of Japan. Alec hears Mister Dixon say, 'More than a thousand Russians out of their element, drifting in downward fashion to the sea bed.'

And the Englishman's reply: 'Doesn't bear thinking about.'

◆

We began to notice
variously
attempts to ascend the greasy pole

In Rouen, a barber held his head under a bowl of water
while his 'assistant' stood by with a stopwatch

In Leigh, a piqued ex-Royal Guardsman sacked for inattentiveness
entered his fifth day of standing upright

In America
a white horse dived from a sixty-foot platform
into a tank filled with water

In Paris, 49,999 guests
sat down to lunch in le Galérie des Machines
to a banquet organised by *Le Matin* newspaper
Nine miles of tables, 3500 waiters
165,000 plates and 13 tonnes of food were provided

A Midlands toolmaker swallowed a two-pound bag of nails

In a pub garden in Kent a beekeeper
entered his fourth day
of staying buried alive

In Paris, a young man hoping to impress
a young woman
crashed
into the Seine on his paper wings

From Dublin, a vegetarian set off to cycle to Persia

It amused Jimmy Duncan. Over his plate of mashed potatoes Jimmy
shook his head.
'You really have to wonder, don't you, what hunger burns in their
souls.'

But this was our milieu — men who would swallow nails.
Lone cyclists, their front wheel doggedly searching east.
So, what was our trick?

In the 'Cock and Bull' over pints of Guinness
to the greengrocer's daughter Freddy Roberts tries to explain.
'Really, it has all to do with space, finding new ways through.'
The greengrocer's daughter smiles. She's taken a shine to Freddy.
She strokes her finger around the glass rim.
'If you get my drift.'
'No. All right
Let me put it this way.
Nope. Better still. Here's what we do.
Let's say you and I go for a short walk.'

She led the way to a lightly wooded area and Fred demonstrated the
various ways through —
the course of a spooked hare
the path of angling light in the trees
then, as it happens — as Fred tells it —
in the new dusk
the sky turned black and quivered

over the spired rooftops
as a flock of starlings
switched shape and direction.

'That's another thing,' says Freddy
'Think of us as fifteen sets of eyes
pairs of hands and feet
attached to single
central nervous system.'

But she wasn't really interested
not really.
She asked Freddy if he could kiss her —
was it allowed, he thought she meant
and pictured Mister Dixon emptying his pipe
and its faint disapproving clatter.
She had to ask him again
'Can I kiss yer?'
And after they did that she asked him to write
'Freddy Roberts' where he kissed her
because she had seen his name in the paper.

Fame's arrow

four

how we
think

<u>four</u>

We visited the great universities. At Oxford, a tiny warden in an enormous black hat walked ahead with a lantern and led us through courtyards with grass so beautifully tended that we wanted to roll around in it like happy dogs. 'So,' said Jimmy Duncan, like this was what he'd been looking for all this time and might even have passed through these gates years earlier had he known about it. In some of us that possibility expanded and contracted.

Cunningham who knew a bit about masonry ran his finger over the stonework.

Hunter who had planted a garden on the family farm got down on his haunches to dig his fingers and test the quality of the mulch.

Tyler who knew all about line from his boat-building knelt to draw the bead of the lawn.

Mister Dixon horrified us all by walking across the lawn to sniff a rambling rose.

Jimmy Duncan banged out the contents of his pipe on the path then seeing our woebegone faces gathered up the blackened ash and tobacco remains and stuck his hand in his pocket.

Billy Stead gazed with longing at grass greener than Southland.

We stood back and admired these squares of lawn framed by ancient stone walls with ivy climbing up from lovingly prepared rose beds.

We thought back to our own shabby grandstands and poorly drained fields. It wasn't as if we lacked for the same elements.

We had rock.

We had flowers.

Decent enough turf.

We had space and light.

But at Oxford what we realised was this —

it was a matter of arrangement, of

getting the combinations right, and of

questioning why we thought something should be this way and not that way,

in other words, a matter of directing thought and a pair of hands

back to a guiding principle.

When we considered the shape of our game

we saw the things at work

that we admired and cultivated

every man's involvement and

a sharing of burden and responsibility.

When we considered the shape of our game

we saw an honest engine.

'Even men who have played rugby since childhood and grown grey in its service could not help expressing astonishment. It was all so dumbfounding, so bewildering, almost uncanny . . .' We did score thirteen tries so we supposed the *Oxford Times* would say that.

'It was an even game,' said one wit, 'because six tries were scored in the first half and seven tries in the second half . . .'

After the game we had dinner at Trinity Hall where we sat at long wooden tables beneath arched windows. On all sides of the dining hall figures of importance bore down upon us, robed men, former scholars, wardens, sirs, bishops, and 'Jacob Hall — rope dancer and acrobat' who was more our thing.

At Cambridge, Steve Casey was pointing with his fork when suddenly the doors to the dining hall were flung over and in marched a dozen male students. They formed a line on the far side of the hall and then turning to face us, raised three loud cheers and each drank down his pitcher of beer, banged them down empty, and, like that, left the hall in a tidy line, their faces filled with accomplishment.

What was all that about?

The Professors looked up from the table or wherever they had turned their thoughts for the duration of the episode and plied us with polite and easy questions —
where were we from?
how were we enjoying England?
had we seen Buckingham Palace?
A thin-faced Classics Professor cracking open a hard-boiled egg with the back of a teaspoon, turned to O'Sullivan: 'Ah, yes, your war dance. Are you aware that it bears an uncanny likeness to Achilles' war cry, you know, in the opera, *Priam?*' O'Sullivan did not know that.

But that wasn't all that we didn't know. At Oxford and Cambridge there were inscriptions with Roman numerals that we could not decipher, bits of ancient language chipped out of rock that we did not recognise, statues, busts, columns, and life-like figures from stories that we either did not know or had only half-heard.

Our industry was football and experiments with space.

What we knew
what we understood
had no beautiful language at its service
lacked for artists and sculptors
what we knew was intimate

as instinct or memory

Our knowledge hinged on the word 'like'.

We could say that, that tree there
is like
our beech
or that woman's eye
caught between secrecy
and full disclosure
is sloped
like
a fig

Or we could say 'like'
when we needed time to think
what it was exactly
that needed explanation

'Like' was the hinge
on which unknowingness swung into light
we could say 'like'
when we meant 'imagine this'

For example, Billy Stead describing our 'pleasure principle' to a
newspaperman —

to glide outside a man is
like
pushing on a door
and coming through
to a larger world
      a glorious feeling
      like

science
sweet
immaculate
truth

Space was our medium
our play stuff
we championed the long view
the vista
the English settled for the courtyard

The English saw a thing
we saw the space inbetween
The English saw a tackler
we saw space either side
The English saw an obstacle
we saw an opportunity
The English saw a needle
we saw its mean eye
The English saw a tunnel
we saw a circular understanding
The formality of doorways caused the English to stumble into one
another and compare ties
while we sailed through like the proud figureheads we were
The English were preoccupied with mazes
we preferred the lofty ambition of Invercargill's streets

Billy Stead laughed up at the ceiling. He'd been making these points
to the newspaperman and had just thrown in Invercargill to see if he
could get the hometown into the Cambridge newspaper. Now, at the
behest of the reporter, he set about describing the various character
of space —

the come-hither appeal of that space between the Plimsoll and the ever-flattering surface of the ocean

the upturned wagering ends of the turf between Billy Wallace's sprint for the corner flag and the diagonal run of Billy's opponent desperate to shut down the space

there was the dare of the tightroper who of necessity imagines air to be solid

there was the fox outside Cambridge which he'd seen turn and run this way and that, in and out of the hounds pursuing it — a life-saving understanding of space instantly lost to memory

there were the trails of a life spent in a valley

and the distance travelled between obscurity and fame

<u>five</u>

homesickness

five

There were idle moments
such as
the hour after breakfast
walking beside a slow-moving river
filled with toast and eggs
not really feeling like victors
kicking bronze-coloured leaves about.
Talk of a kind
'How's that knee, Jimmy mate?'
The bigger blokes like Nicholson, Seeling
walking with the detachment of giraffes.

There were the trains
the endless sitting and looking out the window
at the cows and the passing farmhouses.
On long trips, between Durham and Edinburgh, say,
we got so used to looking out at the world that we forgot our part
in it.
We forgot that we were really bank clerks, foundrymen, farmers and
miners.
We moved across the country and it was like it wasn't really there,
and, we weren't quite in it.

The unquenchable nature of success sat on us lightly
but it meant routines —
Another train, another hotel, another match
Another speech — honoraries, dignitaries, your highnesses, gracious
visitors, His Lord and Lady, the Mayor and Mayoress, ladies and
gentlemen
Mister Dixon reaching for the same old card — 'Far be it for me to
comment on the quality of the opposition we have yet to meet . . .'
Toasts, and more toasts
then off into the night with old injuries and new ones
black and blue bruises
the rockabye sway of the horse-drawn wagon
our tired silence
the strange voices that called to us from unseen doorways in the fog
a baby's cry sending Stead's thoughts to Invercargill
the scrape of a shovel in the coal box fetching Corbett and Cunningham
a dog's bark causing the ears of Deans and Hunter to twitch
and the exact hour in the hills registering in their eyes.

West Hartlepool. After a month's absence we found ourselves at the
edge of the sea. Booth announced the apple and apricot trees around
Alexandra would be coming into blossom now. Dave Gallaher got out
his sister's letter and read aloud a description of her 'first swim of the
season' and of the 'salt drying on her arms'. Our thoughts turned
homeward, to Mission Bay, fruit salad and the smell of hot sand. We
remembered old sunburns, the first plunge off the end of the jetty.
Our first kiss. That first parting of the flesh. We thought of these
homebaked moments, noting the difference between them and this.
In West Hartlepool it was cold and grey, the sea had been spread with
a knife and we shivered inside our skulls. Even Mister Dixon who, at
times like this looked to ward off homesickness with a clap of his hands
or a song, fell quiet. Then Jimmy Hunter broke the silence. 'How's this,'

he said. 'In Mangamahu, on a hot day, the gorse bushes explode.'

◆

Mangamahu. In frigid Scotland a word didn't come any more exotic than Jimmy Hunter's patch.

For some of us Scotland meant going 'home'. Billy Stead pictures himself knocking on an old wood-splintered door in Girvan. For now though he sits in the carriage practising reef knots with his boot laces, pulling one end then the other, seeing how well his Maori and Ayrshire strands knit together. Part of him is going home. Part of McDonald and Glasgow. Part of Jimmy Duncan. A lesser part of Freddy Roberts. A smidgeon of Seeling and Tyler.

◆

At Edinburgh we stepped from the carriages to the cheers of 300 New Zealand and Australian medical students. We waved and shouted back at one another across the divide of tracks and steam. A lone brisk Scots official found Mister Dixon and pointed the way to where the transport from the station awaited us. Through the shifting vapour and steam we looked around for the dignitaries. Well, what do you know. Edinburgh was the first town where the Mayor failed to meet us.

Scotland was the only union in the United Kingdom to refuse us a guaranteed sum ahead of the match. The Scots had lost money on the Canadian tour the year before and didn't want to invite the same again. So, at Inverleith, we would split the gate. The Scots had not foreseen the fame that rolled out ahead of us, and all week the English newspapers had poked fun at them for offering us the gate; now the Scots looked to retaliate in a variety of petty ways.

We heard that they planned to play a mystery formation against us. We heard they would not be awarding their players 'caps' as they did not regard the match as a 'true international'.

homesickness

Thursday night we put our boots outside our door to be cleaned and found them in the morning stuffed with stale bread crusts.

We shook our heads. It would never happen at home.

We spent the day looking over the city, visiting castles, fountains, busts, and stamping warmth into our feet.

Saturday we woke to a freeze and news that the Scots had failed to protect the ground with hay.

That would never have happened at home!

Then the Scottish captain, Bedell-Sivright, in the company of an official, turned up at the hotel to suggest we call the game off as the ground was rock hard and possibly dangerous. So Billy Stead, Mister Dixon, Jimmy Hunter and Billy Wallace went off with the Scots to see for themselves.

They found the ground was already packed with cold spectators. The crowd seemed to sniff out thoughts of abandonment in the Scottish pair, and seeing Bedell-Sivright prod the turf they began to chant — 'Play! Play! Play!' We had no thoughts of denying them and after we said as much, Bedell-Sivright gave a stiff nod and marched away with the official. We shook our heads and pretended to be amused.

But we knew, didn't we, it would never happen at home.

◆

The noise of the turnstiles clicking over did give us pleasure.

◆

The Scots niggle hadn't yet finished. They wanted 35-minute halves; we wanted 45-minute spells. Then the Scots insisted we provide the match ball, but of course we had not even thought to bring one to the ground. The Scots officials shrugged and sighed and looked lost. Jesus H! We shook our heads with disbelief.

It would never happen at home.

In the end, a shapeless ball was squirrelled up from a dusty corner under the stand.

The game was late starting when one of the horses bringing the Scots' wagon to the ground skidded on ice and fell over; there was a delay until another horse arrived, and because of this, there was no time for the traditional team picture to be taken.

As the Scots were led out by a pipe band we noticed their boots had been fitted with 'bars' like those that ice skaters wear. We wore our customary studs — by the end of the game our feet were a mess of blood blisters.

The Scots won the toss and kicked off. For the first ten minutes we were all over them like a mad dog's rash. Fred worked the blind and Billy Wallace dashed over in the corner — but he was called back. The referee ruled the pass was forward. Fred stuck his hands on his hips and glowered. He'd never thrown a straighter pass. Moments later George Smith was clear, the line ahead, when the whistle went for another alleged 'forward pass'.

The referee strolled around like a farmer with his crook making his way through a herd, without hurry or urgency, and was seldom placed to appreciate the shape of our game.

The Scots made little effort to attack. They either hugged the touchline or stood in the pockets of our backs. The penalties awarded us were of no use. We couldn't dig a hole in the ground in which to place the ball for a shot at goal. Billy Glenn, who was linesman, produced a pocket knife for Billy Wallace to dig a hole, but the Scots objected to the practice, so Dave Gallaher had to spread himself over the frozen ground to hold the ball upright for Billy to swing his boot through.

The Scots played three halfbacks against us; that was the *mystery formation*. The bigger surprise came when they started the scoring — Simpson potting a field goal; the unshapely ball wobbled through the air and scraped over the crossbar. The Scots were up 4–nil and for the first time in nearly three months we were behind on the scoreboard.

Minutes later, Billy Wallace lays on a lovely raking kick cross-field to find the Scots corner flag. Billy is admiring his work when he's hit by a late charge — his legs fly up and the frozen ground receives his head. Shadows and shapes of all kinds drift in and out of Billy's brain. As he comes to, the first words he hears are, 'You all right, Bill?' 'Jesus no, I'm not,' he says. Helped into a sitting position he rubs his eyes and sees O'Sullivan and Gallaher in a heated exchange with one of the Scottish forwards.

Our reply came with Seeling taking a long throw to the lineout and charging upfield. In the tackle he places the ball for Glasgow to kick past Scoullar, the Scottish fullback; Scoullar has to turn and run back and Frank wins the race to fall on the ball over the line.

We were keen to build on that score, but the icy ground took away our feet. We couldn't feel the turf. We couldn't prop without our feet sliding out from under.
Instead, we did it by numbers. From a scrum near halfway Fred threw a cut-out pass to Jimmy Hunter. Thereafter it was just a matter of procedure — drawing and passing, Jimmy to Bob Deans with Smithy's finish in the corner.

Our 6–4 lead ended following a stupid mistake. A ball from a lineout on our line went loose. Two of our players diving for it contrived to knock each other clear and a Scottish forward fell on the ball.

The Scots went to the break up 7–6 and this was another new experience for us. Behind at half time!

The Scots sniffed possibility. The crowd too. They forgot it was freezing.

You saw them smiling past their red, dripping noses. The crowd was roped off but the Scots officials marched up and down the sideline shouting encouragement to their boys.

The loose cannon who flattened Billy banged up our forwards as they leapt for lineout ball, but if we retaliated the crowd hooted. Nothing was going our way. The Scots defence got in the way of our back play. We could hear our boys in the stand yelling out to us — 'Ten minutes! Ten minutes to go! Open it up!'

Four minutes to go we put down a scrum on halfway, fifteen in from the sideline. McDonald and Glasgow won us a clean heel. The Scottish halves, as they had done all game, rushed Fred and Billy Stead. This time Fred threw a lovely dummy and went alone. On an angling run he finds Bob Deans who draws and passes to George Smith, and with soaring hearts and grinfuls of pride we watched George cut infield and swerve out again leaving the last Scotsman on one knee, his hands spread over the cut-up turf. Downfield George carefully placed the ball between the uprights. My God! It was a beautiful sight.

In the stand the medical students were on their feet and yelling. Between the shouts we heard the creeping silence of the Scots.

We carried little George back to halfway on our shoulders.

On the stroke of full-time we picked up bonus points after Cunningham fell on a loose ball over the Scots line, and that was more or less it. Heartbreak at one end of the field. Joy at the other.

In the changing shed Frank Glasgow let the air out of the ball; he'd folded up the leather and packed it away with his kit when a Scots official arrived to demand the ball back. It was our custom for the man who last touched the ball to keep it. We explained this to the official.

Gallaher waded into the debate. 'Hold on,' he said. 'There seems to be some confusion here.' To the Scots official he said, 'We are the guests here. At least, I think I'm right in saying that.' And he looked around for support. 'Boys? Am I right?' 'We are the visitors,' someone said. 'But in Scotland it doesn't necessarily mean you are also guests.' The Scots official closed his eyes. Two heavy lines appeared where his eyes and mouth had been. In the end, Frank said, 'To hell with it,' and threw him the piece of leather. We told him, 'This would never happen at home. I can tell you, mate!'

We dined alone that night.

Sunday. We woke to a skin of ice on the windows and turned over in our beds and went back to sleep. Our feet were stiff and raw from the ground at Inverleith. After lunch we rode in drays out to the Forth Bridge but could not see anything for the fog. The freezing conditions sent us back to the hotel. That evening we spread ourselves before a blazing fire and rubbed away our aches and pains with a special lotion —

Eucalyptus   . . .60 parts
Whisky   . . .30 parts
Hartshorn   . . .10 parts

Mister Dixon's diary

'Glasgow. Again the Scots snubbed us. No show from their officials. People from Queen's Park Soccer Club made up for it. Laid on professional trainers who poured hot baths and rubbed the boys down after the game. Only 10,000 in the crowd to see us beat the West of Scotland 22–nil. Heavy ground and a cold wind. Tries to Freddy Roberts, 'Dunk' and Smithy. That evening the Queen's Park officials put on a musical evening, and later, escorted us down to the train station. Arrived late in the evening at Ardossan and boarded the ferry to Belfast.'

A black night crossing. We lay in our bunks smoking and talking,
and drifted off to thoughts of home. Nothing specific, or sometimes
specific —
The dog, for example
or a favourite chair
a bed from childhood
a favourite pipe
eyes tearing at the memory
of the world-can-wait smell of bacon fat
popping in the skillet.
High in the hills a fresh wind
that faint smell of deer.
The walk to the window that precedes
the sharing of indelicate news —
someone's death
a shotgun marriage —
and looking out at the back yard with its chore list:
this work-in-progress
that keeps its own time, manages its own routine
has never been to Europe or anywhere else
but the back yard
and wants to know only those stories
it has seen and heard for itself.

◆

We woke in Belfast and in the dark boarded a train to Dublin. From
the station we swung round Dublin's streets in a dozen 'jaunting cars'
and at the Imperial Hotel picked our way through a large crowd. The
hotel manager had set aside a large room and the hundreds who'd
welcomed us outside now swarmed through the doors. Cards of
introduction were pressed on us. Simon Mynott took a card advertising
window-cleaners from a short man with a shining earnest face. 'Have
you winders down dere in New Zealand, son?' A poet who hired out
his best lines for headstones pressed a card on Mona Thompson and

said, 'I try to get to know the individual . . .'

Breakfast was a long time coming.

That night we attended the Theatre Royal with the Irish team; as the teams entered the audience stood on their seats and cheered and cheered until they were hoarse.

◆

Friday night we lay under our covers, pinching fleas and listening to the rain.

◆

Saturday morning. We pulled back our curtains to fog in the windows. Dave Gallaher didn't show up to breakfast. He banged up his leg in Scotland and it had got worse. Jimmy Duncan decided Dave should stay back at the hotel. It meant bringing George Gillett in from fullback to occupy Dave's wing forward role and moving Billy Wallace to fullback. We didn't have another fit three-quarter, and so, glancing around the breakfast room, Jimmy Duncan's eye fell on Simon Mynott. 'Can you spare a moment, son . . .?' Simon brings his teacup down the table and Jimmy breaks the news to him. Simon says, 'But I've never played wing,' and Jimmy says, 'Then it'll be a whole new experience, won't it?' He and Billy Stead drew a pattern of wing play on a table napkin and McGregor told him to run up and down a hallway to get used to the idea of the winger's lines of attack.

With Dave out of action, Billy Stead took over the captaincy and we ran out as follows —

                     Wallace
        Smith   Deans   Mynott
            Stead   Hunter
                      Roberts
    Gillett (wing)
            Casey   Tyler
        McDonald   Cunningham   Seeling
            O'Sullivan   Glasgow

Drizzle continued to fall.

A huge punt sent the ball over the grandstand into a Dublin back yard. Another ball was found but this one exploded after a scrum collapse. Waiting for a third ball to arrive we mingled with the Irish players. The Irish fullback Landers jogged upfield to chat with Billy Wallace. Billy Stead and the Irish half looked over folded arms into different sections of the crowd. George Smith grinned at the feet of his Irish opponent — both of them with their hands on hips and legs in an ungainly outsplayed stance, like farmers familiar with each other's problems. Tyler and the Irish hooker, Coffey, moved warily around each other. O'Sullivan and the Irish loosie leant on their respective knees and stared at the ground while picking mud out of the soles of their boots. The tall locks Hamlet and Wilson grazed in the same space as Seeling and Cunningham.

This peaceful scene was interrupted by the arrival of a third ball.

We freed up Jimmy Hunter. Jimmy'd have been across but slipped just short of the line.

After that the Irish came at us with renewed purpose, a mad glint in their eye, pitchforks in hand, ball at the toe. The huge crowd of 40,000 roaring at their backs.

At times it felt as though we were playing two different codes. We saw the paddock as an ever-changing pattern of lines. The Irish, on the other hand, saw the field as a sort of steeplechase, covered with low barriers and walls which as far as they were concerned were there to smash into. They believed in luck. They were like kids taking it in turn to kick a pebble down a bumpy road.

We longed to tell them what they were doing wrong.

We worked our way down to a lineout on the Irish twenty-five. George Gillett won us good ball from his unfamiliar wing forward position which was shifted with quick hands to Bob Deans. Deans dropped his left shoulder, and drawing the giant Basil MacClear in that direction, wrongfooted him, and moved off in the opposite direction to score beneath the crossbar. It was a tidy piece of work from Bob; but Bob being Bob looked a bit guilty about the deception and the flush in his cheeks was a rush of sympathy for MacClear who'd been obviously stuck in the midfield to stop such an eventuality.

In the second half, the wind behind us, we ran at the Irish. Freddy Roberts and Billy Stead in tandem breached the defences and Bob picked up his second try. He couldn't bring himself to look at MacClear as he jogged back from the try-line.

The final scoring moment saw Alec McDonald peel off a scrum to score handily by the uprights and Billy Wallace convert for the final score — 15–nil.

◆

That night we ate at the Gresham Hotel, and Irishman and New Zealander were placed side by side. In speech after speech the Irish said we were the finest bunch to ever take the field. We were magicians. We'd given the ball eyes and ears and taught it the basics of our language. We were irrepressible, a force of nature; they, a fallen leaf with no will of its own. Mister Dixon raised an eyebrow at Gallaher. It was true. The Irish charmed our hides off.

A final toast, and as glasses and tumblers are raised Billy Wallace finds
Billy Glenn, who, raising a white napkin to his lips, nods back.

Part of Billy Wallace and part of Bill Glenn are returning 'home'.

Outside in the cold stinging air they climb up into a jaunty car and
swing through the Dublin night for the train station. They arrive just
as the train to Londonderry is pulling out. They sprint across the
platform and crash through the doors of a reserved compartment.
The wooden gable of the station passes in the top of the window, and
flushed with champagne Billy Wallace looks up from the floor. A man
with a thick bristling moustache and several chins is looking from
one to the other with a postcard in his hand. His companion nods
over his shoulder. 'I'd say dat one dere is Billy Wallace. And the other
is Bill Glenn.'

◆

Londonderry. 1 am. Billy Wallace looks out the carriage window. A
few people are waiting on the platform, among them his relatives. He's
never seen these people before in his life but at once he recognises
them. It's like seeing how he will eventually look when he's very old;
and not so old. As he steps on to the platform his father's father and
his father's brother crush him on both sides. They hug him then hold
him at arm's length to look at him. One sees a son and the other sees a
brother. Billy sees his origins.

The next day rain falls in long thick beads down the windowpane.
Billy's grandfather hasn't seen his son (Billy's father) since he was
eighteen years of age. There is so much to tell. The questions come at
him all day long. Then when his father's schoolmates arrive on the
door the questions start again. Questions about his father and about
the country he's made his life in; soon Billy finds himself giving the
one answer, descriptions that seem to cover both the place and the
person — quiet, warmish, given to long silences, the contentment of
lakes and the way they reflect their surroundings. Billy looks at the

homesickness

folds of his grandfather's face. The old man is grinning down at the pipe he is packing — 'So is ee a good worker, Billy?'

'The best.'

'The best.' His grandfather looks behind to one of his father's old schoolmates. 'Did yea hear dat? The best. Not just "good". No. The best.' He smiles in a secretive way and turns back to Billy. 'So, tell me. How does ee spend his Sunday mornings?' Billy has to think about this. It could be a trick question. He isn't sure whether the old boy is a churchgoer or abstainer. Either way he's bound to be a zealot about his choice. Billy looks up from his teacup. 'I'm sorry,' he says. 'What was the question?' His grandfather leans forward with a cagey grin. 'I asked how my boy spends his Sunday mornings.'

'Thoughtfully,' answers Billy, and this time his grandfather rocks back and slaps his leg with delight. He finds Billy's uncle smirking in the corner of the room. 'Did you hear that?' Now the uncle is shaking his head; his eyes are watering with mirth. The grandfather refills Billy's whisky glass. 'Thoughtfully. I like dat. I like dat a whole lot, Billy.'

The hours pass. Family lore. One or two photographs. Now for some history. The grandfather shows Billy his firearms collection. He picks up an antique weapon, and as he runs his fingertips over the smooth cherry stock his grandfather tells him: 'Dat was used back when Londonderry closed its gates to the English. About two hundred years ago. A relative used dat to kill King James's explosives man.'

'Really?' says Billy.

The old boy purses his lips. 'No. But you can tell that and no harm will come. The next part I'll tell you is one hundred percent true though . . .'

'The next part' he shared with Bill Glenn on the train back to Dublin. 'The siege lasted over a hundred days and people were reduced to such a state they ate dirt and gnawed on hides to stay alive. A dog's paw sold for five shillings!'

'Really?' asks Glenn.

'I'm not entirely sure, Bill, to be honest.'

In Dublin they meet up with the team and hear about the rout at Limerick. We cut Munster apart with five tries, but at a terrible cost. George Smith is carrying his arm in a sling and we have England next.

◆

9 pm. The slick dark of the road leading down to the docks where a huge crowd had assembled to see us to Hollyhead. We stayed out on deck, sharing the freezing night with the crowd, and as the ferry departed they threw their hats in the air.

We were back on water, back to that indeterminate space that we had first liked across the Pacific then grown sick of across the Atlantic. We retired to our cabins and to kill the hours Mister Dixon called for an exchange of 'things never before seen or experienced'. Fats Newton lay on his pillow, his feet up against the cabin walls, and recited his list —

olives at the Irish dinner

street lamps glowing through the bleak London fog at noon

champagne

elephants (in Regent's Park)

a ride in a motor car

black people and Spaniards

Maria George in *The White Chrysanthemum*

The huge swimming pool at Montevideo, all enclosed, two hundred and twenty dressing rooms

on Fats droned —

solid ice over a football field (at Inverleith)

A large wave slapped the porthole and a memory of the Pacific storm tore through us. Into that dark pause Mister Dixon spoke, surprising us all with a list of his own —

shouting Spaniards selling raisins from their rowboats (in Tenerife)

the spume of a whale off the coast of Uruguay

Freddy Roberts's dive from the upper deck of the *Rimutaka* into the clear water of Santa Cruz harbour (Tenerife)

Then he said — 'The look on Emma's face in the window when we said "goodbye" at the wharf,' and no one had the instant reply we would have hoped for.

None of us could think what to say. No one could guess at this new thing that revealed itself in the face of Mister Dixon's wife.

It was an uneasy moment. Then George Tyler spoke up. George said he'd seen a cabbage tree growing out of a rowboat.

'Where might that have been, George?' It was Mister Dixon, and we silently congratulated George on disengaging him from that mysterious look on his wife's face.

'The platform at Saltash Station,' said George. 'It was as we came through . . .'

'Pennycomequick.' That was from Seeling. He spoke slowly, careful to place the emphasis so we were in no doubt where the humour lay. Then, to ward off Mister Dixon he added, 'That's the name of the station near Plymouth. Pennycomequick.'

Booth laughed but shut up at once when he realised he was alone.

Jimmy Duncan rolled off his bunk and stood up; once there seemed to not know what to do with himself.

Then someone said 'Sleep' and off we trailed to our dreams.

A cold and dirty London day
We smoked our pipes and gazed at the windows
An inordinate amount of yawning
The click of billiard balls
The horsey neigh of Dave Gallaher appraising his poker hand.
Our 'lazy day' before the match against England

On match days we had our special routines
Some liked to go out for a brisk walk
Gallaher to find a beggar to tip for luck

Freddy Roberts to find a wall to throw a ball against

Massa Johnston liked to lie in a deep bath and look up at the ceiling cracks

Jimmy Hunter drank one pot of tea after another and peed nervously

Simon Mynott pretended to chew in public even though there was nothing in his mouth

O'Sullivan lay on the floorboards of his room

Fats Newton and Bill Corbett swept the remains of breakfast from the plates of those too nervous to eat onto their own plates

Mister Dixon checked the team tobacco tin was full

Billy Stead and George Nicholson set up shop in the corner of the hotel kitchen or rooftop, whatever availed itself, and laid out their trade instruments — pliers, new laces, Nugget, Dubbin, sprigs, some gut thread and needles of varying length and width. At their feet, a sea of boots in matching pairs, left and right toes appealing to them

We left the hotel in Aldersgate Road at 10 am to avoid the traffic. An hour later we were wandering across a heavy and boggy Crystal Palace field.

Some of the boys shuffled off to the pavilion to look at the Egyptian and Ottoman displays. Jimmy Hunter and Billy Wallace sat in the stand, Billy's eye noting the goal line at both ends, the angle of the posts, placing the ball here and there in his mind's eye.

A line of impoverished-looking trees stand on three sides of the ground. They are different from the stricken ones Jimmy Hunter's seen in cleared land around Taranaki. There the trees left standing are white as bone and bear the shape of surrender. The trees around Crystal Palace have simply shed their leaves and in the dull light the sooty branches look drawn against the sky, as if they've never known a decent wind to blow through them. And as Jimmy's looking, he sees the branches move. He doesn't say anything to Billy Wallace; doesn't want to interrupt his flow. Now, squinting into the distance, he can make out a number of small figures crawling along the branches. One at a time, like a bead of water off a sill, they drop from the ends of the branches overhanging the ground. A cap fell off one and as the man bends to recover it suddenly Jimmy can see hundreds of them. Hundreds are climbing the trees and dropping over the fence then picking themselves up. In another direction he can see the top hats of the crowd moving slowly along the fenceline for the entrances. The entrances are too few, and as the lines back up more and more people are climbing up those trees. He's watching them, small as ants, when the sound of a bellbird echoing from afar, across oceans, has him looking past these English trees to the heavily dressed branches of an elm brushing back the hurrying brown water of the Wanganui; the elm and the water, home and a girl he knows, and about now, Eric Harper presses down on his shoulder, and says, 'It's time, Jimmy Hunter.'

◆

In our tiny changing shed
our thoughts turned to all that glass above
and the weight of silence

We found comfort in our routines

The noise of the players banging their pipes
The team bowl filling with cinders and ash

Now the hanging up of pipes
The tucking in of shirts

Now stamping warmth into our chilblain feet
'Gentlemen,' says the official at the door

Freddy Roberts spins the ball through his fingers (Freddy, as always, like a dog at a gate)

George Gillett, apart, stares off to a distant sunny day

Deans fussily folds his trousers along the crease

Billy Wallace smiles at what he already professes to know

'Right then,' says Gallaher, his lead-dog eye picking up each one of us

'One final thing,' says Jimmy Duncan. 'Remember who we are.'

We'd beaten the Scots.
We'd beaten the Irish.
We told ourselves, 'We must not lose.'
We told it repeatedly — 'We must not lose' —
until it began to sound like a direction.
'Go to the end of the street but there you must not turn right . . .'
It had its own logic. Its own ring of truth.

But at 2.45, when we walked out to the pitch and looked up and saw all those people, our hearts dropped. No one had ever seen a crowd like it. In the stand the tall hats of the gentry; to the sides of the stand the numbers were packed in, up and down the banks, and across the field we saw figures on the skyline, perched on the ends of branches, others hugging the trunks. And who were we they'd come to see? A bank clerk clutching his leather headgear, a couple of farmers, a farrier, a couple of miners and a bootmaker.

We looked to Gallaher for a lead. We saw his gaze circle in a smaller space than that which had threatened to overwhelm us. He clapped his hands, winked at Freddy Roberts, gave Frank Glasgow's shoulder a pat, said to Billy Wallace and O'Sullivan, 'Don't forget what those

homesickness

English bastards did to your Irish forebears . . .' One by one Dave
patched us up and by the time of the national anthems we were back
intact.

◆

The English tactic was a variation on the Irish one of deploying the
giant Basil MacClear in the midfield to create a kind of log jam. The
English stacked their backline with five wing three-quarters.

They hadn't thought about the blind side, though, and while they
guarded the front entrance we ducked down the alleyway, Freddy
Roberts scampering crossfield to draw the English wing and flick on
to Dunk McGregor who crossed for four identical tries. The second
one saw Billy Stead draw the winger to create the space for Dunk. The
English were so slow to catch on we shook our heads in disbelief. We
told ourselves, 'You'd think they'd know by now.' The English didn't
seem to know what to do. They scratched their moustaches and tried
to look bemused. It could have been worse for them. Deans got across
but was called back for a forward pass from Jimmy Hunter. Then Billy
Wallace was over but the referee judged that he had knocked on.
Debatable. Highly debatable. Still, it didn't alter the outcome. A greasy
ball and the inability of Billy Wallace to kick out of a bog saved England
from an embarrassing halftime score. It was all a bit too easy. In the
second half we went about our work. The loosies dribbled over the
line for Fatty Newton to score a soft try. Shortly after, Dunk followed
up with his fourth try, this time on the end of a good pass from Deans
in open field.

The newspapers praised our 'wonderful passing — the best ever seen
with such a ball on such a heavy field' and noted the almost 'corporate
instinct' of our pack. 'They played like eight men with one eye, and
that an all-seeing eye . . .'

◆

It was our last game in London and 75,000 people stood as one to cheer us from the field.

That night we were fêted under the glittering dome of the Alexandra Room at the Trocadero and souvenired the menus —

Consommé Sarah Bernhardt

Queue de boeuf licée

Turbot d'Ostend

Sauce hollandaise

Selle de mouton Niçoise

Salade romaine

Ris de veau

Poires Melbe

The toasts and speeches came between courses.

'Your Worships & other dignitaries, His Lordships, ladies & gentlemen . . . please be upstanding . . . to toast the greatest team to ever visit England's shores . . .'

homesickness

six

fatigue
and the
irresistible
attraction of
defeat

six

Was there ever the time
to do anything other
than march under the banner
feed the horses
see to their shoes
sharpen weaponry
and make sure everything was in good working order?

We had Sunday afternoons
'down time'
on the edge of the Serpentine, say
smoking our pipes
and watching the ducks ski on to the ice
on their orange plaid feet.
Despite the comical spectacle
the ducks did not appear to crave a crowd —
there was no scoreboard, no tally
no one particular touchdown sticks in the memory.
The ducks simply came in and took off again.
Came in and took off again.
They were ducks, and
content to be ducks.

On to the Hippodrome
to see ' "Savade" in the silvered grille with his lions
tigers, bears & dogs
ALSO
Fishing Cormorants.
A real demonstration of the art of fishing.
Real Cormorants from the East.
Real Chinese fishermen.
Real water.'

We grew tired of who we were
the way complete strangers advanced with an outstretched finger.
'You're 'im, aren't you.' The stranger's face lighting up. 'It is you.' Then,
turning to his friends with his discovery. 'Look who I've got here. It's
him.'
The way their ruddy faces closed in and trapped you with their pints
held to their chests to talk about the game against Middlesex, say.
'That Jimmy Hunter . . . he's a cheeky wee bugger . . .'
A tall man with a parson's nose enquiring after Glasgow's weight: 'I
hear ee's seventeen stones. Can that be right?'
The unexpected way that praise could drag on the heart. 'Thar Billy
Wallace. I mean the man's a marvel. Jackett don't move like ee does.
Jackett's a corpse compared to your Billy Wallace.'
The difficulty of transactions in the public gaze; at last you've caught
the publican's eye but when he asks, 'What will it be then?' the
drinkers chorus, 'No Stuart, good God, man. You don't ask this man
to pay.'
To be pulled from our seats in the audience — 'Ladies and gentlemen,
we have with us tonight . . .'

To be summoned by a wealthy farmer needing our opinion of his apple
cider. It was good, but 'good' wasn't the word he was after.
'A glass of water is good,' he said, so we upgraded 'good' to 'the best
we'd ever tasted'.

Halfway through dinner his daughter made an appearance. We gazed at her for she was the most beautiful of creatures.

Eric Harper tried to make eye contact. Frank Glasgow coughed for her attention. But the daughter did not appear to see us. She only saw her father. There were no introductions. At a nod from the farmer she disappeared as she had come without a word or glance for us.

'And now,' said the farmer, laying down his mutton knife, 'I have one or two paintings I would like you to see . . .'

The way others sought you out to lecture you.
Savade the Lion Tamer comes to mind
with his long black boots and silver hair
and grand moustache, and
the casual way he laid his whip in his lap.
The way he and his lions seemed on the brink
of sharing an ear-splitting joke.
He had asked some of us back following his show.
We were offered a sweet green tea.
The lion tamer said he'd seen us beat England.
So, he had been at Crystal Palace.
Did he enjoy the game? Did he understand what he saw?
Yes. Yes.
But now we saw him drag a finger along his moustache.
'There is just a question about the presentation.
I wonder if I might advise you on crowds,'
and for the next five minutes he spoke of their character, how they worked.
'It is not so much what you do but how you do it . . .'
He asked Jimmy Hunter to demonstrate the act of scoring a try.
Jimmy said he would need a ball so a small sequinned cushion was found.

Jimmy spins it in his hands, and after he has jogged around behind the 'posts' to place the cushion the lion tamer pushes himself up from his lion tamer's chair. 'Jimmy, I have a suggestion. May I have the cushion.' Jimmy flicks him the cushion as he would to the flying Booth or Wallace. The lion tamer does everything Jimmy did, only after placing the cushion he thrusts out a finger to each section of the crowd. North. South. East. West. Shouting at us, 'Bring the crowd into it whenever you can. Share your joy.' Then his arms fell at his sides. 'It is only a suggestion.'

One of the acrobats who had been watching now took the cushion and after placing the 'try' launched into a series of amazing backward somersaults. The lion tamer was scathing. 'We are not trying to add wonder. We are exploring ways to work the crowd!' The acrobat sloped away with an injured look. To Jimmy the great Savade was more solicitous. 'Jimmy, I hope you don't mind my . . .'

'No, no,' says Jimmy.

The Bohemian tightrope walker was next. After scoring the 'try' he snapped his feet together and raised his arms as if to enter a swallow dive. The lion tamer closed his eyes and muttered under his breath, 'Thespian.'

Now it was the clown's turn. He ran a short distance, placed the ball, then ran open-mouthed to each section of the crowd. The lion tamer folded his arms and stifling a yawn slid down in his chair. 'I am not moved. Are you, Jimmy? Mona? Billy? Dave? No, I thought not.'

Finally it was the ringmaster's turn but his effort was so funereal it didn't warrant a comment.

Lorenzo, the failed juggler, could not place the 'ball'. Each time he tried to his foot got in the way, and so on . . .

◆

Having no space to call our own
we began to hunt down monasteries
and castles
to slip down an ancient alleyway
and sink back against centuries-old stone
and close our eyes

relieved to orbit in our own little world
as bootmaker and foundryman.

◆

Two days after victory over England the crusade moved on to
Cheltenham and the familiar din of carpenters' hammers rushing to
put up temporary stands and the familiar Sunday dead of schools and
businesses closed for the big occasion. We did that — we changed
people's lives just as the abnormality of an eclipse saw flowers close
up in the mistaken belief night had fallen. In the hard light of the
empty street you saw shopkeepers blink, and the stretched faces of
grinning children. There was the familiar emptying out of the
countryside. The new timetabling to handle the load. Trains arriving
from as far away as Birmingham, Bristol and Cardiff. At Cheltenham,
for the first time we heard the high-pitched sing-song of the Welsh
come over the border to get a look at us.

We did our thing and in the morning left for Birkenhead. At midday
we presented our shop-worn smiles at a reception hosted by the
commercial men of the Stock Exchange.

We ran all over Cheshire and the local newspaper wrote: 'Individually
[they] were incomparably superior. Collectively they were ridiculously
superior.' But we knew that, and our dulled eyes looked for something
new. At the station the Cheshire boys turned up to see us off. As the
train doors began to close, they felt in their pockets for something to
give, then tore cufflinks from their sleeves.

We arrived in Leeds to glorious weather and another huge crowd on
the platform.

The goodwill gestures and promises made at the last stop washed off
us as we made new acquaintances. On the field we bagged ten tries
and sloped off to the train to meet another itinerary.

◆

Then, the long journey from Bradford to Cardiff
Yawning in the dry carriage air
The sound of a water cracker breaking; Tyler brushing crumbs off his
lap
Jimmy Duncan banging his pipe on the window sill
and all those tiny moments that fill in departure and arrival — cows,
hedges, grey slate roofs, grey slate cottages, the usual talk —
'Leg all right?'
'Ribs in good nick?'
'Knee coming right, is it?'
'Organise you a cup of tea, shall I?'

We got out our old letters, opened them up at their creases
and reread our favourite passages — to do with home
the old school house, washing lines, goalposts, and kite-flying —
that time she held the string in her teeth to tie on a ribbon

Those who sat back with eyes closed enabled others to note the strain
on their faces; the poultice over Gallaher's neck boils; Smithy half-
turned in his seat to protect his injured shoulder; others with crook
legs dangled into the aisle, the flesh hard and swollen around the
infected area that had still to be lanced.

Our hospital train silence.

When we looked up again, England had passed into Wales.

Mister Dixon leant across Corbett's folded arms to clear a circle in the
misted window, and through it passed the shingles and boards of
Newport's businesses — tobacconists, collieries, herbal remedies,
biscuits, tailors and laundries.

Wales. This is how Wales arrived in our window. With a squeal of
wheels locking, followed by a hiss of steam. A single figure raced by.

Then another. And as we came to a halt the figures in the window appeared to go backwards. Then in the condensation on the glass you saw a man's wild eye, someone else's mouth; and like a quarter moon stood on its end a woman's face and her mad delight. Fists pounded against the carriage and the window. We heard our names being yelled out. Our names in the mouths of folk we didn't even know. As we began to move out and a hand clawed the window we found ourselves wondering about this mad human undertow — on what did it feed?

George Nicholson turned away from the window with an ashen face. In the top third of the glass a line of yellow lights clicked by, then the night came and we sat back. Mister Dixon with his timepiece in his hand. Jimmy Duncan staring blankly down the aisle. Some of us took out our tobacco then did nothing with it except to let it lie in our lap.

We had heard that the newspapermen had gathered from every corner of the Kingdom, some from as far away as the Continent.

We heard it said that if the Welsh beat us the players would never again want for medicine, food or a roof.

From travellers we heard about the Welsh kneeling their children before their beds to pray for victory.

Wales. We were too tired for Wales.

◆

We pulled into Cardiff just before midnight. We braced ourselves for a repeat of the Newport scenes but as we hobbled out to the platform with our suitcases and football boots there were only officials waiting to lead us to the drays and horses. Billy Wallace swung his kicking foot at a moth.

The sickest of us drew back to that quiet cave within and counted numbers or did whatever trick worked best to make the time go

Fatigue and the irresistible attraction of defeat

between the station and Queen's Hotel in Westgate Street.

The ambush came in the poorly lit streets around the railway station. We were half asleep, our chins bobbing against our chests, when they flew at us with their goblin language. They reached up wanting to touch us, shouting and shoving, and we had to pull our legs clear from their grasping. The front horses fought with the reins, twisted their heads and the bit. The startled face of Thompson looked back, then he disappeared around a corner and the space between filled with people shouting and waving.

The horses reared up and we saw the white terror in their eyes. We saw the clenched faces of the police wrestling the crowd back, and we held on to our seats with grim smiles.

A crowd of twenty thousand was later mentioned.
But can that be right? That many?
What did a man say to his son or wife?
'I might just pop down to the station to see if their train's come in?'

◆

Away from the delirious hearts and famished stares we discussed what it might be that they desired.
Steve Casey recounted this incident — he had been enjoying his soup in the Loaded Bull when he'd looked up to see a pigeon tapping its beak and thrashing its wings against the window.
Says Steve, 'You can see what is going on in Mister Pigeon's head — the soup urn with its floating bits of crab and mussels is just there the revolving cake stand with its butterfly cakes is just there.
Everything you could ever want is just there almost within easy reach but for that window pane.'

◆

The Welsh had not lost at home for six years.

◆

Wales v New Zealand

result   result   result

Half-time and Final Score

telephoned and telegraphed to any address

for one shilling, sixpence. Reply promptly — Owen,

12 Church Street, Cardiff.

---

advertisement in *South Wales Echo*, December 13, 1905

We heard later . . . they turned up in their droves, men and women of all ages, some elderly on sticks, mothers with infants who tied prams to the railings to get their message to Dai to read when the coal hulk got in to Skye. The front door to Owen's place stayed open all afternoon through the night to the early hours. People said you entered a front room and found Owen bent over his desk, papers and ink. People queued from his front room, along his hall, out into the street and down as far as Westgate. Some with the advertisement torn from the newspaper. Others glancing up from the address written in the palm of their hand. No two instructions were alike.

A man sailing for Faroe asked the result to be telegraphed to the Department of Revenues in Lisbon. Lisbon was two days' travelling time from Faroe and he wanted to receive the news as new. But also desiring an element of suspense he asked for the half-time score to be followed a day later by the full-time result.

A number of wedding parties in the north requested half-time and final scores to be phoned through during the later toasts.

Fatigue and the irresistible attraction of defeat

There were numbers for Prague, St Petersburg, Russia; Sydney, Australia; New Zealand of course; a Welsh doctor/missionary working in Leopoldville, Africa. Port Said was another, the customs office there; one of a bridge party heading for Port Said had played on the wing for Neath.

A house servant all the way from Bristol asked for a full description of the match to be telephoned through to his employer — the information should include scores, those involved, and in addition, those promising moves that otherwise came to nothing.

A young mother with a baby clinging to her side told Owen her 'dae's lungs'd collapsed'. He was to telephone his wife who would walk the result five miles to the tuberculosis ward in Swansea. She said, 'You can cable the result as requested but I can tell yer, I knowt my ma will tell me dae that Wales won, regardless.'

The Great Western Railway Company laid on thirty extra trains. The first to pull in were from the West of England.

Then at 10.40 am the Ogmore and Garw Valley contingents arrived. They were followed by people from the western valleys of Monmouthshire, from Weymouth, from Birmingham, Liverpool, Swindon, London, Paignton.

Between 10 am and 1 pm another fifteen trains arrived with folk from the Rhondda Valley. Still more arrived at Rhymney Station — trains from Llanidloes via the Cambrian Line. People from Abergavenny, Merthyr and Aberdare . . . and so on, until the valleys had emptied out and there were just women and small children left.

❖

Our hotel sat across from Cardiff Arms, and from about mid-morning at an upstairs window you could pull back a curtain and see the crowd muster outside the police barriers. You saw them walking along and reading their ticket of entry — just to be sure. Men in cloth caps, buttoned-up suits and heavy boots. In twos and threes, or large numbers from a particular mine or village, or a man on his own with a coat draped over his arm, in single file they entered Westgate Road. Some were too excited to smoke and allowed their cigarettes to burn down to their fingers. Their heads nodded at conversations to which they weren't really paying any attention. Faces swollen with calculation looked anxiously to where the bank was filling up by the second.

A woman later wrote about her village after all the men left. She said:

1. You noticed the journey of clouds more
2. Women sat together on their porches picking the dead skin off their calloused feet
3. Great distances fell upon roads which had fallen quiet
4. The younger beauties gave up lowering their eyes and could be heard swinging on long ropes across the river past the second bridge leading out of town

Then, the hour before the men came back:

1. We sat in houses staring up at cobwebs in unreachable places
2. Outside, on the street, the cobblestones stiffened
3. On Sunday, we slaughtered our pigs

We had an early lunch. Some of us stared at our plates. Simon Mynott who had been picked ahead of Billy Stead stirred his food around with a fork. Duncan McGregor and George Gillett kept getting up to go to the toilet. Mister Dixon dipped his head to taste the soup then must have sensed he was alone; he looked up and finding the rest of us staring at our plates he set his spoon down, pulled the napkin from his collar, and pushed his bowl away.

At 1.15 we walked across to Cardiff Arms and our pavilion. Billy Wallace brought up the rear and a section of the crowd that happened to catch sight of him roared like dogs. Billy shut the door behind him, his back pressed against it, like he'd just got in from atrocious weather.

We regrouped and lit our pipes and listened to the band's programme of music —

March	– The New Colonial
Overture	– Lad Diademe
Selection	– Reminiscences of Wales
	Jeunesse Dorée
	Hen Wlad fy Nhadu
	Heavy Cavalry
	Life of a Soldier
Polka	– Des Clowns
Selection	– Reminiscences of England
Troop	– May Blossom
Fantasia	– Welcome, Brother Jonathan
March	– Grand Imperial

Then —

Land of My Fathers

at which point the crowd joined in.

Instinctively we glanced up to the rafters and the shifting space between gable and iron.

Those of us who could not make a comparison sat spellbound.

What a fright we were to Jimmy Duncan's eyes.

He banged down his pipe. He got up and began to pace up and down.

We were nowhere we hadn't been before, right?

Right, says Jimmy to his own question.

Think back to Crystal Palace. Was that a crowd or what?

Inverleith. They wanted you boys stewed and served up on toast. They wanted your balls battered and fried. Am I getting through?

So, listen. You know what Wales is doing, right now?

I'll tell you. They're thinking about us. They're thinking about a team who's arrived on their doorstep with 801 points for — and just the 22 against. Don't tell me they aren't quietly shitting themselves. Don't tell me . . .

No one did.

We stood up and all of us stared at the door, each waiting for the other to open the damn thing, till Jimmy Duncan muttered a profanity.

As we left the pavilion for the team photo the singing picked up, louder than anything we'd heard before, as though a section of the crowd had deliberately held back. Now as we entered more fully into view their mouths opened wider — Wales! Wales!

During the singing of the national anthems the Welsh team did not look at us but to a holy place somewhere between the crowd and inside their hearts, their mouths moving slowly and tunelessly.

On their own they began to sing *Sospen Fach*, and the whole crowd stood as one to sing with them.

We stood in a line facing them. Our shoulders touched, and we thought back to a sleet-filled day on Wellington Harbour.

If you looked to the rear of the vast crowd you saw an easy breeze stroke a light smoke from the chimney tops. Ground conditions were good. It was a perfect day.

◆

So what happened?
First, the excuses —
a rising injury toll
fatigue

fatigue and the irresistible attraction of defeat

poor refereeing — the endless persecution of Dave Gallaher for every imaginable offence, until Dave told the front row they weren't to hook: 'Better they have the ball than a free kick.'

We could even put it down to curiosity:

we knew all about winning but what did failure feel like?

We pushed on that door — we pushed a little harder than we needed to.

Or we could blame it on our failure to change.

We had stopped being original.

At the first scrum we saw the Welsh adopt our formation.

Wherever we looked we found a mirror image of ourselves.

How did it go now?

dum de dah dum de dah bang whooshbang whoosh clicketty click bang

Our music, only to Welsh names —

Owen feints to the open side and goes the blind, sends the ball on to Pritchard, Bush, Gabe and Morgan who flies for the corner.

The ball slickly changing hands and Morgan crossing our line without a hand laid on him. It was as if we had swapped jerseys.

We hadn't known defeat. We had no idea that it had a shape to it. Or that past a certain threshold there was no way back. At lineouts the forwards avoided eye contact. Newton with his hands on his knees. O'Sullivan's eyes came over heavy-lidded. Gallaher looked fed up, hands on hips, head cocked to one side then the other.

The magic spark that enabled Simon Mynott to carve up Cheshire has flickered out. Now he looks ordinary, mishandling the ball, misdirecting kicks. Time and again, anticipating a touchfinder, Billy Stead has run along the touchline with his flag only for Simon's kick to stay in play. Outside him a bewildered Jimmy Hunter stares at his numb hands. They seem incapable of holding anything thrown to him. For three-quarters of the match the back three of Gillett, Wallace and McGregor look on in frustration and disbelief.

◆

'Everything must be done at speed otherwise the value of the movement is lost.' How often did we hear that from Billy Wallace?

Sixty minutes into the game a lineout forms on our side of halfway. From a long throw-in the Welsh gain possession and break through; seeing Fred in their way they kick past him a loose and aimless kick. The ball rolling with a left-to-right bias. The Welsh charge after it, changing course as the ball does, their shoulders touching. Now Billy Wallace comes off his wing, scoops up the ball and cuts across the face of the oncoming Welsh forwards. You could freeze the moment and countless others like it, from street games of pick-up five-a-side, to similar half-chances flowering at Thorndon Primary School, through to club rugby and all those tropical hours spent with Billy Stead theorising and arranging the quoits on deck.

The Welsh backs are spread. Billy lines up the midfield, then straightening between Nicholls and Gabe explodes into space. He's through with just the fullback to beat. Winfield is on the twenty-five, his arms spread ready. Then Billy Wallace hears 'Bill! Bill!' He draws Winfield and pops the pass to Deans.

From the moment he started his run Bob was aware of the Welsh winger Teddy Morgan shadowing him. Now the breath and the soft thud of Morgan's feet ghost in his ear. He can keep on the diagonal, running farther from Morgan, or he can straighten up for the shorter course that'll bring him alongside the posts. He straightens up.

Along the near touchline Billy Stead is sprinting with his flag yelling at Bob — it's not an instruction or anything really, just release, pure joy as Bob goes over the line in Morgan's tackle. Backfield Gallaher mouths a silent 'yes' in the direction of heaven. Mynott is catching up wth a shy smile. Gillett walks towards the Welsh line with his arms raised. A huge grin stretches Tyler's muddy face. Seeling and the rest of the boys rush forward to congratulate Bob.

A word here about the crowd. They were silent. We had experienced something similar that time George Smith broke the Scots' hearts at Inverleith. We knew silence in all its guises —
the silence of English hotel lobbies
the deathly night silence which is broken by a horse's snorting
the tongue-tied silence of forests
the silence of icebergs and awe
the silent language of clouds over oceans
the conspiring hand signals of haystacks
some of us knew about the silence that can fall between a man and a woman
and the timeless silence that collects inside domes

The Cardiff Arms silence we would later recall as 'a form of evidence'.

Deans is spread-eagled, his chin on the ground. His eyes sting with sweat but he can just make out the wreaths of silence up and down the Cardiff Arms embankment.

Now the voices of Seeling and Tyler arrive singularly. 'Bob. Bob. Bob . . .' At different moments it sounds like 'thanks' or it's a 'you bloody beaut' kind of sounding Bob.

Then, weirdly, the ground begins to slip away from under him. He's being pulled back from the line. Someone has his legs, someone else has his jersey, and it's like a sitting-room wrestle where you struggle for every inch of the rug. 'Hey. Hey. Hey,' he says. His arms are outstretched so that the only part of him touching the ball are his fingertips, then they too lose contact and the ball is left on its own like an island receding into the distance with fond memories and 'adieu, adieu' hanging over it.

About now we picked up a different register in the crowd's silence. It began to shuffle and become uncomfortable with itself. An unravelling of silence, if you like. The referee arrived on the scene, slipping and sliding in his street shoes.

Over at the touchline Billy Stead is leaning forward the way you do at the edge of a lake factoring in unknown things. The scene on the field has become confusing. Players are talking and arguing.

Owen, the Welsh half, is gesturing to where the ball has been laid. And now the referee points to the ground where he wishes to set a five-yard scrum.

The silence of the crowd broke then as several thousand relieved voices find one another.

We put down the scrum under the Welsh posts and after Bush found touch the crowd resumed their seats with a variety of embarrassed looks.

The game moved on to the final quarter with us launching ourselves at the Welsh line. We ran at them with a kind of blind terror. Now we had an inkling of what defeat might be like we were desperate to avoid it.

On one occasion, Simon Mynott was held up over the line. Simon tried gamely to wriggle through and it was like watching a sheep try to free itself of fencing wire.

On another occasion Fred went to the blindside and found Duncan McGregor who ran like a spooked deer. He went over in the corner but before we could throw up our arms in triumph the referee pulled him back for a 'forward pass'.

Then the whistle went
The whistle went
The whistle went and we hadn't won
We had lost
They had won

The whistle went and the 45,000 Welsh invaded the pitch. We were picked up and swept out the gates into Westgate Road. From time to time we caught glimpses of one another. Gallaher shoving down on Welsh shoulders as if trying to make his way along an overgrown bush track. Jimmy Hunter helpless, one hand raised, caught in a fast water. Newton shoving against it. Bob Deans looking like a man deep in argument with himself.

In ones and twos we found our way back in to Cardiff Arms. Once we'd all assembled we walked across to the Welsh shed to offer congratulations. Every minute or so another Welsh player arrived with a stunned or joyous look and Gallaher shook his hand. O'Sullivan greeted each one with a 'Well done.'

In our shed Seeling lay back in the tin bathtub, his eyes closed, his weary arms resting along the bathtub rim. McDonald threw his boots down and pulled his socks off any-old-fashion and dragged himself to the bath. No one mentioned the referee. No one uttered his name. No one mentioned what we'd heard in the Welsh shed. A reporter asked Morgan if he thought Deans had scored and over the slap of water had come another of those silences that you don't forget. We sat in our tubs and found ourselves smiling with grim hearts at Morgan's clever and evasive choice of words: 'I'm too elated to go into details.'

We crawled out of the tubs, dressed and dragged ourselves across the road to find the doors of the hotel flung open. The hinges had come loose. Police were everywhere after a rampant crowd had run through the bar. It was like a storm had hit.

We dragged ourselves upstairs to our rooms where we fell on our beds.
Defeat.
It was the emptiest and most confounding of feelings.
Feeling may not be the right word because none of us could testify to feeling anything. We'd lost all feeling — in one shot then the rest through a slow seepage.

You're on your way to your wedding when you hear that your bride has changed her mind. She's had a change of heart. You grin. You look out the window of your carriage. There is the countryside, more strange and distant than ever before. You look for help but instead find everyone looking back at you, and asking you over and over, 'How do you feel? How do you feel?'

We met on the landing to go down to the dinner. Mister Dixon fixed his tie in the hall mirror until we were all accounted for. No one said a thing until Jimmy Duncan spoke up while going down the stairs. 'I'd'ave accepted a draw. A draw would'ave been right. A draw and you wouldn't hear a peep out of me.'

We sat down to eat with the Welsh the following items —

Oysters

Consommé à la Princesse

ෙ🕊

Fried Smelts, tartare sauce

Boiled Turkey, chippolata sauce

Welsh Saddle of Mutton

Wild Duck

Salade à la Française

ෙ🕊

Orange Jelly

Nesselrode Ice Cream

◆

Sunday morning. Bill Mackrell lies in bed, listening to the gurgling in the downpipes and the silent run of the night rain in the guttering. He's sick again. For three months he's been sick. He arrived in England feeling sick. All across the Kingdom he has looked up at different ceiling patterns and counted the cracks. All night he listened to the Welsh passing beneath his window, singing, carousing, drunk in their language.

fatigue and the irresistible attraction of defeat

Now, outside his door he can hear his own kind. The monotones of Bunny Abbott and Eric Harper. And that's George Tyler. That's Frank Glasgow. That's Alec. He can hear them going down to breakfast. He can see them as he would were he in the same room —

Dave Gallaher with that fasting stare of someone sitting at the back of a crowded hall

Jimmy Duncan will be on his feet. They won't get him into a chair, not today they won't, not while that fleck of irritability rolls about in his eye

Mona'll be kicking doors

Bronco most likely the same

George Nicholson looking on from the edge of group despondency; not quite part of it but wanting to be

Mister Dixon, like God, finding different expressions for every conceivable moment

The refusual of Jimmy Hunter's gaze to travel beyond the tip of his nose

The downcast look of Billy Wallace; privately prohibiting himself to smile, but sullenness not finding a peg either

The solid porcelain object Tyler's face becomes when that near-permanent smile is tugged from it

Alec? McDonald's the only one he can see with a newspaper open, buttering his toast as he reads the match reports

Newton's probably there with him, a napkin tucked into his collar, and in deference to the circumstances shoving the sausage to one side

◆

'It was the first defeat of the New Zealanders whose long sequence of victories had established with them such a habit of winning that it was difficult to realise that they had at last experienced defeat.'

◆

Defeat took us back home and we saw in our different ways where we lived and the effect on that place that the news had —
the way the small houses appeared to move back from one another
men sat through church services completely deaf and unable to speak.

Much later, when we caught up with the mailbag in New York, we heard how the news appeared to affect natural phenomena.
How clouds in strong winds were seen to come to an abrupt halt.
A bird thought about flight, changed its mind, and appeared to drop like a rock.
A brown column of smoke from a distant scrub fire appeared to lose all heart and was seen to drift earthwards in a tumbling staircase of white and grey ash.

None of us could imagine laughter again except as something that might happen to other people.

Smiling Welsh officials turned up with drays and drove us out to Penarth. It was three miles through wooded countryside to the coast. We passed the day walking out our bruises and aches along the shore and skipping flat pebbles across the tidal flats.
We had lost heart. Lost interest in the Crusade. Now we'd lost, what was there to defend anymore?

Recognising the problem, back at the hotel we returned to our shipboard games. Mister Dixon shook a handful of dice and came up with a suggestion. 'Why don't we try inventing a place where there's no such thing as fame. No one's ever heard of it.'

Eric Harper's eyes followed a smoke ring to the ceiling. He said, 'A place where there's no mirrors.'

'Or portrait galleries,' he added.

'Crowds are never known to assemble.' (McDonald)

'There are postcards but they're only of natural stuff, flora, the odd bird perhaps.' (Mynott)

'No one knows you except as somebody's son, brother, cousin, or in-law.' When Jimmy Hunter said that we all looked up at the same moment. This wasn't a mythic place at all. It was nothing of the kind. We'd just described 'home'. And the notion of that collected in our faces like an ocean wave crashing ashore.

Two days after the Cardiff Arms Test we turned up to play Glamorgan. Tries to Bunny Abbott, Alec McDonald and Billy Wallace — Billy off a nicely weighted kick through from George Smith who was back briefly from injury. A gale blew across the ground and it was impossible for Billy Wallace to find the uprights. We had hoped for better things. We'd hoped to put the Cardiff Arms misery behind us, but on the eve of the match twelve of the Welsh internationals withdrew, and while Glamorgan fielded a weakened side we sensed in the crowd their wonder at what the fuss was all about. We looked no better than ordinary.

The Times stood by us and gave the 9–nil victory 58 lines, 34 more than the article on the 'defence of Australia', 28 lines more than strikes leave 'Moscow in Darkness', and 52 more lines than the Prince of Wales' attendance at an Indian military display of 'elephants and bullocks employed in drawing guns'.

We returned to Cardiff and spent the Friday playing billiards and thinking about Newport.

Now that we had lost we felt we could safely do it again and nothing would happen.

On the field we couldn't decide if we wanted to be there or what it was we were supposed to do.

There were momentary flashes of old form. Harper scoring on the end of a pretty passing move. Mona came close before he was tipped out in the corner. But our confidence had gone. Everything we did took a crucial second longer than it had before Cardiff. Jimmy Hunter's wonderful corkscrew runs were now demonstrated by a man who couldn't decide which door to go through. Speed of hand required speed of thought but we'd lost that. We'd lost our confidence to be 'who we were'.

Billy Stead, who was captain for the day, had to bully Billy Wallace into having a long-distance shot from a penalty awarded near halfway. The great Carbine is in a pessimistic mood. He says, 'No, I can't do that.' And Billy says, 'You won't know until you try.' And Carbine says, 'I know what's possible. I know it like I know I can't hold my head underwater for ten minutes.' Meanwhile the crowd is sitting in its silent thousands trying to follow this discussion. Finally Billy says, 'Give it a go anyway. Have a dropkick.' So, reluctantly, Carbine turns the ball in his hands feeling for its inner shape. The rest of us stand back, hands on hips, heads tilted back to watch the ball sail between the uprights.

Still, no one spoke of grace anymore. It was like it had been rubbed from our limbs. In the changing shed we were a muddy ruin.

The Times judged us accordingly with 48 lines, ten lines less than the article on 'Christmas Dinners to the Poor' — 'Each family of five and upwards received 5lbs beef, $1^1/4$ lbs suet, a quartern of bread, $^1/4$ lb tea, 2lb sugar, 1lb raisins, 1lb currants, $^1/4$ lb peel, 2 oranges, and a flag for the pudding . . .' Still more than that given to the debate on the number of Jews killed in Odessa; and a description of the fighting in Moscow.

◆

Fatigue and the irresistible attraction of defeat

Christmas Eve we spent walking the Cardiff streets looking in the festive windows and wishing we hadn't spent all our allowance.

◆

Christmas Day. Corbett woke with boils on his neck. Smithy's shoulder was playing up again. Bill Mackrell lay in bed coughing. Gallaher was unable to straighten his leg. The back of Freddy Roberts' hand was black from a stomping. A poisoned area on Steve Casey's back needed lancing.

We limped down to Christmas dinner, toasts, crackers, bonbons, cigars and coffee. We presented Mister Dixon with an umbrella engraved with all our names. Each of us received a Christmas card and a portion of Christmas cake neatly packaged in a small china bowl from a Mr and Mrs Clifford of Blenheim, Marlborough, New Zealand.

We stayed in that evening. Bob Deans led a small church service. We stood in a circle and the flames from the fire cast shadow and light over our faces and made our silence devout, and Bob intoned for us, 'God be in our thoughts and in our words . . .'

◆

Boxing Day. Fifty thousand packed into Cardiff Arms. We sat in our shed with our pipes while the bloodshot crowd roared out the song to commemorate Teddy Morgan's try in Wales' victory.

Jimmy Duncan got up and looked angrily out the door. Whoever was more or less fit filed past Jimmy out to the middle where the Cardiff players in their hooped jerseys stood waiting for us.
Within minutes of the start, O'Sullivan broke his collarbone and we played the game a man short, Dave Gallaher switching to the front row and Frank Glasgow to Sully's place on the side of the scrum. Dave's move to hooker took him out of view of the crowd's heckling. With

Dave hooking and Billy Stead feeding the scrum we won more ball than we knew what to do with.

We should have been first on to the scoreboard but Deans failed to take in a long ball from Jimmy Hunter, and the honour instead fell to Cardiff. From a lineout Gabe drifted through our lines to hand on to Nicholls who crossed over unopposed. It was too easy, too sweet, heart-breakingly close to what we had done throughout the months of September, October and November. Then when the conversion struck an upright and clumsily dropped over the crossbar the glances of the big men especially — Nicholson, Seeling and Glasgow — sunk into the mud at their feet.

Near half-time Mona Thompson ran on to a flat ball from Deans and went over in Winfield's arms in the corner. That part of the field was so densely packed that the spectators had to stand and move their chairs back to open a lane for Billy Wallace to line up his conversion attempt. A spectator coughed as he moved in but it made no difference. The ball spun through the uprights and Billy had his hundredth goal on tour.

Midway through the second half, a dribbling rush saw Seeling kick past Winfield. He and Nicholson gave chase as the ball rolled into the dead ball area. Bush who was back covering had plenty of time to force the ball dead. He had all the time in the world, so much time that he thought he would look up and appraise the situation. As he did so he saw Nicholson and Seeling bearing down on him, panicked, took a fly kick at the ball, missed, and Nicholson 'gathered in that ball as if it had been a long-lost sweetheart' to score.

Hurray. Hurray. We limped back across Westgate Road with a two-point win.

They said the better team lost that day. We heard it all night and the next day. We saw it written in the newspapers and on the faces we passed in the streets of Cardiff.

◆

Three days later we fronted up to play Swansea — our thirty-second match.

A wind howled down the field. The spectators huddled next to each other with eager faces. We felt the weight of their hope. The very wind bore it into our faces. For twenty-five minutes Swansea pounded our line before scoring. Duncan McGregor quickly replied for us. But, but . . . no. The linesman has raised his flag. He is pointing to where Dunk put a foot into touch. No, no. Surely not. The ground had been covered with hay to protect it against frost and when we cleared it away to find the touchline we discovered Duncan had been inside the field of play by several yards. By now, however, the ball was adjudged 'dead' and the try was lost to us.

We changed around at the half down 3–nil. We had the wind at our backs but were too exhausted to make much use of it.

Billy Wallace proved the difference. Our last scoring moment in the United Kingdom comes as Billy fields a line kick on our halfway. He juggles the ball in his hands, sways back from the touchline. Now he starts infield on an angling run. The rest of us are looking on with detachment and a sense of possibility — wondering is this a lone mission or will we be called on to help — when Billy lets fly with a field goal off his left boot. His left boot! From that angle and in those winds!

The crowd rose and it was like their tongues were wrenched out. They looked at one another. Billy Wallace had done it to them. Billy had saved our tucker.

They mobbed us at the railway station. They shook our arms off.

Slapped our backs. They liked us after all. When the train pulled into Cardiff twenty minutes later, another huge crowd were waiting for us. Their faces crammed into the window. They sang *Sospen Fach* through the glass and we rocked the carriage with a haka. The Welsh followed up with another song and we stomped our feet for another haka. And as the train moved off towards England we fell back in our seats dead with exhaustion.

◆

For our one-point win over Swansea
The Times gave us 75 lines, longer than
'the crisis in Odessa is over'
longer than 'the suppression of the Moscow Revolt'
longer than 'St Petersburg strike at an end'
We'd done our bit and held on to our reputation

Throughout the night, at railway stations across England, men, women and children waited up to cheer us as the train came through. They lined the station platform and threw their hats in the air. Nodding in and out of sleep, we woke to cheers and urged one another to our feet for another haka. Then as the train sought the darkness of the countryside we fell back into our seats and pulled our hats over our faces and tried to sleep.

At 4 am, we chugged into Paddington. We staggered out with our boots and suitcases to be met by a line of station porters who threw their caps into the air and raised three cheers.

We got in a few hours' sleep in the Great Western, then it was back on to the train for Folkestone, the boat, the English Channel and France.

seven

overseas
experience

seven

Women? Parlez-vous français?

There was Freddy Roberts' greengrocer girl to whom he introduced ideas of space and longing

George Smith and the Irish widow

George Smith and the lion tamer's daughter

The chambermaid who drew the outline of her mouth on an apple which she placed outside Steve Casey's door

The French waitress whose eyes turned corners

The Glaswegian kitchenhand who sent Frank Glasgow a love letter in the shape of a heart concealed in his egg yoke

The Irish widow

The Dorset widow

The proposals that arrived in the mail — 'I am five foot two inches and weigh eighty-six pounds . . .'

Mister Dixon's insistence that they answer every letter

The destitute Glaswegian widow to whom Bob Deans gave twenty-five pounds when we passed around the hat to buy her a washing machine so she might take in washing to earn her keep

The way women isolated us to whisper in our ears — 'Are you the number 3?' — when they thought you might be George Smith and how, after looking around to make sure George wasn't about, we always answered, 'Yes, I'm he, I'm your man'

The wives of officials who moved like ships leaving their berth, a rustle of skirts, a hand presented

The French girl who stuck her tongue down George Gillett's throat
The cheeky theatre girls we met backstage who sat on our laps
whispering disgraceful things
Mister Dixon's blind eye
The wink in Jimmy Duncan's
The night-time assignations

The lonely path back through the park to the hotel; and the boys
milling outside the hotel steps in the distance: Massa with the
newspapers, Mona in his bowler hat, Jimmy bowing his tea cosy head
to light up his pipe, Cunningham in his black seaman's jersey with
the ribbed collar blowing hot air into his big hands, Freddy Roberts
with one foot up on the step, hands in pockets; the way they appeared
to move together, like a herd bound by a solid core that knows and
only wants itself for company.

The things that women later wrote or shared with newspapers: 'They
were hopeless at fielding a compliment. In a crowded room they sought
the walls and looked for doorways . . . They drank too quickly. I said to
him once, "No one is going to take your glass," and he just looked at
me, then at the glass in his hand. Like I said, "slow charm".'

Winter flattened the fields right to the grey walls of farm cottages.
Out of that scene Paris arrived: between looking down and up again a
whole city appeared.

Paris was caught in a freeze.
We stood outside Gare du Nord, stomping and breaking up the ice
and watching the cabbies try to pick up their fallen horses.
Our ears pricked up at the names we heard — 'Anand, Suzette,
Catérine'.
The horses looked prettier than ours.

We decided we liked Paris.

We liked it for not being Wales or England.

We especially liked the way women in the streets kissed men on both cheeks.

We thought we could get used to that.

There were no brass bands.

No officials.

No policemen on horses.

No gaping crowds.

There were the usual snail and frog jokes & jokelettes; lively discussion on what we were prepared to eat and what we would point blank refuse, and so on. Corbett, usually a retiring debater, made violent gestures of swiping the tablecloth and throwing down his table napkin in disgust outside the Gard du Nord.

But that evening at dinner, we found ourselves making odd announcements; Cunningham, for example, waving a slice of tomato on the end of his fork and declaring, 'Now this *is* a tomato.' But we knew what he meant; Corbett, Glasgow, Newton, nodding, their mouths too full of tuna flakes and oil and chopped spring onions for them to speak.

Mister Dixon treated us to cognac, and afterwards, in the lounge of the St Petersburg Hotel, we smoked our pipes and drifted off until some hours later we woke to him standing over us, frowning at the timepiece in his hand. Then he looked up and his face burst with a big generous smile. 'Boys,' he said. 'Welcome to 1906.'

◆

New Year's Day we breakfasted in bed, spoke a pissabout Maori/ *franglais* and used up all our 'mercis' and 'beaucoups' to organise a pot of tea since none of us drank 'café'.

Midday we dragged ourselves from bed, shaved, and packed our boots for the car ride out to Parc des Princes. A car ride! It was the second time we'd driven to the park on match day.

It was bitterly cold but a crowd of 12,000 turned up with their white kerchiefs and black umbrellas. Whoever was fit to play pulled on the jersey:

```
                        Booth
        Harper        Wallace              Abbott
            Mynott              Hunter
                        Stead

            Gallaher
            Mackrell              Tyler
        Glasgow       Newton       Cunningham
            Seeling              Glenn
```

The French front row sported beards and as far away as wing and fullback the helpless giggling of our front rowers could be heard.

The ground was a gravel pitch with very little turf.

Bunny Abbott started the scoring. Then the French scored. Bravo! Bravo! We were happy for them. Yes. Cessieux dived over for France and 12,000 umbrellas were thrown in the air. 'Le brave! Cessieux, Cessieux! Un essai, un essai!' The French players did handsprings and hugged one another. We grinned like lizards. Dave Gallaher passed the word round to let the French score again.

The French forwards took play into our quarter, whereupon our backs wandered out of position or looked up at the Parisien skies to help Jerome find space. 'Just before the line he stopped and looked back to make certain the whistle hadn't blown, then dived over.' Again, umbrellas went up around the ground. Waiting on the conversion

Dave said, 'That'll do them,' and we set about collecting six tries ourselves.

◆

We liked the French
We were surprised to discover that we liked the French
We had an inkling that we were not supposed to

◆

overseas experience

The after-match dinner 'offert dans les salons du Restaurant Champeaux' —

Consommé aux Quenelles-Bisque à Ecrivisses

Suprêmes de Barbue à la Dieppoise

Aloyau à la Nivernaise

Faisans sur Croustades
Parfait de Foie Gras Truffé

Salade

Haricots Verts à la Maître d'Hôtel

Corbeilles de Fruits

Vins
Chablis — Médoc
Château Margaux 1896
Café. Liqueurs

Afterwards, we strolled through Montmartre
listening to our alien voices
gauging our mystery.

◆

In Paris — how we liked saying that —
In Paris we visited the sights:
acted the goat along the Champs Elysées
put a scrum down before the Arc de Triomphe
wandered the halls of Versailles
explored the Grand Trianon, the palace
Louis X1V built for his mistress.
We marvelled that a private affair
could materialise
into such a monumental thing.

Here, in the Tuileries, you saw how trees grew
wanting to do their best.
You saw spires
and understood that where thoughts went to
was exactly the same place where ideas were fetched down.

In Paris, we let our eyes wander the fabled skyline.

In Paris, the clouds moved sedately
like debutantes
very aware, we felt, of where they were
as we were.

In Paree — how we liked saying that — in Paree, we saw our own
ideas promoted in art. In England we were celebrated for never
producing the same move twice in a match while in Paree, we saw the
same idea magnificently expressed in the stained glass window of Saint

Champelle where no two panels of glass are alike.

In Paris, we went our different ways —
The loosies went off with O'Sullivan
to soak up the atmosphere
of Place de la Concorde
where the heads of aristocrats had rolled.

A man from Cooks, a scholar of Latin and antiquities
escorted Billy Stead to see the 'green woman' by Matisse
& the Venus de Milo
in the afternoon Billy sat at Emile Zola's desk
picturing the Aegean filled with sailing vessels
their decks crammed with statues — Zeus, Hermes, Apollo roped to a
mast, Diana playing her harp on the bow of an Albanian schooner.

History. It felt good to work yourself into that old story.

George Smith and Eric Harper posed for their photo beside a statue of
one of Napoleon's generals.

Carbine, Massa, Bunny Abbott, Eric Harper and Jimmy Hunter went
off with a horse and guide and came back with a horrific tale of dashed
hope. They were driving along the Seine when the driver stopped the
dray outside a nondescript building. Jimmy says they were expecting
more works of art. But no, presently they enter a room where a dozen
people are sitting around in chairs. It's cold as hell, and already Massa
is looking for the door back to the street. The air is a bit strained. A
waiting-room type of silence. No one saying anything. Bunny says
'Bonjour' to one Frenchman, but is given the cold shoulder. About
then Jimmy notices a stream of water running down the front of those
sitting down. Then he notices that each one is tied to the chair. And
it's left to Massa to burst out, 'They're dead!'

The driver who has brought them to the Paris morgue looks the least surprised. His hands are held respectfully at his sides. His fawn-coloured eyes sympathise with a woman in a nightdress. She has on a hotel doorman's jacket and one slipper. Her foot looks solid, like blue porcelain, and her eyes have the shattered quality of coloured church glass. The director of the morgue, an immaculately dressed man, cane, bow-tie, moved out of the shadows to rest a hand on the woman's shoulder. 'Ma petite chère.' And made a tsk-tsk sound as he shook his head.

In a chair next to her sat a man with a drooping moustache and sad bags beneath his eyes. Bunny thought he looked depressed — as if between jumping, falling and landing he'd changed his mind three times.

'Ah oui,' said the director. A tragic case of an inventor hoping to impress the world and in particular, a young woman from the sixth arrondissement, with a special chemical solution that made short men taller.

It worked! No, listen. It worked but with a depressant side-effect.

They found the spurned lover with the wings. There was a rib of built-up scar tissue where the wings had been attached.

They tiptoed around the other suicides, looking in their faces, searching for clues. Then, it was time to leave; all the way back to the hotel they talked among themselves of opportunities, lost chances and spilled ball. Hearts not really in lunch, apparently.

◆

'Cheerful lot, aren't we?' said Jimmy Duncan, and stood up to distance himself. We were back at the Gard du Nord waiting for the train to Calais. To buck us up Mackrell said he'd seen a pigeon resting on the tipped wing of a sculpted angel. But no one could get their thoughts away from the morgue.

Then Bill Glenn said he'd seen a sailing boat transporting an automobile across a lake.
No one could be bothered with taking this up.
'Quite odd, actually, when you think about it,' Bill said. We could accept that too and sank back into our silence.

Jimmy Duncan, jiggling his pocket change, said, 'You know today I saw a bald man selling eggs.' No one believed him. A bald head. Eggs. A bit obvious, Jimmy. 'Down from the hotel a bit, on the boulevard,' he added, and out of obligation our interest shifted back to Bill Glenn's sailing boat and the automobile. What kind of automobile? How big a boat? Which lake? Until Jimmy said, 'Bugger it, I'm going to go and try some of that French café.'

We slipped back into London without fanfare and with two weeks to fill before we set sail for New York, we went our separate ways —

Billy Wallace up to Newcastle where at Freddy Roberts' cousin's house they recorded 'Tenei te tangata pai rawa atu' on a wax cylinder.

Smith, Tyler, Cunningam and Stead to a Fulham boarding house.

For others, London meant a return to those temporary loves we had met and now needed to say goodbye to . . .

Lori's story
That night, well, we'd been playing with a make-believe future. We'd worked it all out. He said he would become a professional. I said I'd sell flowers at the club gates. He said, 'No fear, Lori. No you won't.' Then he leant over to tap his pipe on the floorboards. He says to me,

'Who'll look after the kids?' I laughed. 'Well,' he said, 'if you're out there selling flowers and everything . . .' I said, 'What kids would they be?' And he answered quick as anything, 'Tom and Beatrice,' smiling like he'd already met them and I should know them too. He caught my eye and we both burst out laughing. Then a funny thing happened. After he fell asleep and I lay back looking up at the ceiling, I began to think about Tom and Beatrice. What they might look like. Red-haired, I hoped. With fair skin and eyes like black coals.

In the morning . . . well. In the morning everything was hurried. Everything we'd said was left behind in the night. There was a rush for the bath along the hall. We left our teacups half-drunk. I lost a glove in the hurry to get to the station. There was just time for a thanks-love-write-to-me-won't-you-peck-on-the-cheek, then the train snatched him from me. I could see them in the windows. And they were smiling. They looked so happy to be on their way. I could see the shadows of those others getting on and moving behind all those smiling faces. I imagine his was one of those laughing and joking. They were going home and it made me sick to think it might be to somewhere better. I watched them. There was a cloud of steam, a burst of the train's whistle, until everything was of itself. The platform. The wooden seats. The withered sky. And my life — as he had found it.

◆

Steaming down the Solent past the Isle of Wight, Cunningham turns to Stead and says, 'You know, it has just dawned on me that corned beef and cabbage are not far off, and I suppose it will be back to the old pick.'

◆

The first night out into the English Channel, a French tender met us off the coast of Cherbourg with '400 emigrants from mid-Europe'.

It was a wild night, the moon hidden by thick cloud and a blinding rain flew at us. Waves hit us beam on.

We were out on deck whacking the dried mud from the cleats of our boots when we noticed the narrow bow of the French tender rise and drop into a trough, and as it rose again tiny voices could be heard. The tender swung the mail across on a wire hawser. After the mail the basket came back with a woman and two tiny girls. The basket hit the rail and the girls spilled on to the deck. Sully and Nicholson were quick to help them to their feet, and the tiny girls stared at them bug-eyed and clung to their mother. Back and forth the basket went. Someone said they were Russians. Someone else altered that to 'Jews'. A third person mentioned Odessa and it dawned on us that two stories had found each other. In the months of October, November and December we'd shared column inches, side by side, in *The Times*, and now we were sharing a boat to New York. The basket went back to the tender and soon after swung on to the SS *New Yorker* with an elderly man clutching a violin. We stared at one another. Us at the violinist's white beard and pink eyes. The violinist at us with our football boots in our hands.

The wind had got up and now a sea washed against the side and tipped over the deck to cries of, 'Get back with you! Get away from the rail!' The basket went back for one more family: two boys and a terrified woman swung out of the sleet screaming in their foreign language. Then the captain said, 'Enough.' We left with families split; some with us, fathers, grandparents wailing into the wind from the deck of the tender.

◆

America. As it came into view we took our place at the rail with the refugees. At Sandy Hook we took on doctors, port officers and customs officers till we were up the Hudson River 'under the shadows of New York's skyscrapers'. Along with the Russians we stared at what we had failed to imagine ahead of our arrival.

We had loosely thought about Indians
Wild Bill, hillocks, bison, and prairie

Time and again, the city galloped away from us.

◆

In New York we attracted a different crowd
Curious onlookers shopping for a game
Professors from Princeton and Yale
A young reporter from the *Brooklyn Eagle*
A group of bank vice-presidents who chomped on cigars at our practice
An officer from West Point, his sabre at ease alongside his striped leg
A clothing company's representatives
A publisher of popular postcards
A boot manufacturer who souvenired one of Steve Casey's

We played New York on a hard baseball field in Brooklyn
or 'Brooklands' as Billy Wallace called it
We lent New York Abbott, McGregor, Duncan, Casey, Newton and
Mynott, and walked and talked the game's finer points on our way to
a 46–13 win.

From England, Ireland, Scotland, Wales and France we carried injuries,
bruises that showed no sign of healing, boils, slow-mending cuts from
areas lanced to release the poison.
Now we passed through America in a haze of fatigue and dream.

In Chicago Billy Wallace and Jimmy Hunter visited the meatworks
which boasted they used every part of the animal except the squeal:
'. . . the pig goes in one end of the machine and comes out the other as
hams, sausages, lard, margarine and binding for bibles . . .'

At the station men with shovels and grain bags and suitcases boarded with their wives and children with red-rimmed eyes and combed wet hair. Swedes, Germans and some Dalmatians. Men who held the handle end of their shovels between their legs for hundreds of miles across an unchanging prairie. How they knew where to get off and why this place recommended itself ahead of any other was a mystery.

We watched them from our window take a deep breath, the men putting on their hats as they turned to face their future.

One woman — she refused to get off. She'd looked out the window and seeing the prairie grass waving in the wind and nothing else but sky and a horizon froze her will.
We watched to see what would happen. Outside, her old man with the shovel looked back over his shoulder, dug in his shovel, and turned his whole slow body round to the carriage door. We saw him say something to the boy. The boy came back down the carriage. We waited to see what would happen. The boy spoke to his mother in a foreign language. He pulled his mother's sleeve. She tucked her elbow in and closed her eyes. Her mouth cut a hard line. She wouldn't look out the window at her old man either.

Finally, Jimmy Duncan got up and went and sat next to her. He said, 'Pardon me,' American style. We watched Jimmy cross his legs and look down the aisle. He winked at the boy, and to the boy's mother he spoke in a gentle voice about the business of arrival, which is something Jimmy could claim to have first-hand knowledge of, the opposition's field, an unfamiliar ref, nasty changing sheds, a home crowd; that, and anxiety for how it will all turn out. Can I do the job? By now the woman was looking at him closely. Jimmy kept firing his words down the aisle. Now he uncrossed his legs and easing himself forward and taking hold of her wrist, he said to her, 'Go on. Take the bit between your teeth. I see your old man and kid waiting for you beside the track. Go out there and make history.'

A week later, in Frisco, we were to read a newspaper account of a prairie woman who'd arrived in town penniless.

She said her boy was bit by a rattlesnake

That was okay, though

Then a horse kicked the side of his head

He'd taken to his bed and not woken up

Then her husband had left — where? she couldn't say

She woke up one morning, the door open to the prairie

and his favourite hairbrush gone

We were still on the train and it didn't feel like we were any closer to home. From England the world just stretched farther west. Distant hills gave way to more plains and start-up towns; then the whole thing repeated itself, hills, plains, start-up towns.

On to Cheyenne where we got off to walk beside the tracks, in night air

so cold it was thin and brittle and stung our nostrils.

We spoke in whispers and stood with our backs to trackside fires.

In the window of the station we could see Billy Stead and Mona Thompson studying their hand in a game of poker with a Polish Count and his former housemaid; they were looking to California to start new lives.

They knew very little about football.

On the long journey west we told old stories, went back over our favourite matches, played cards, emptied our pockets to see what mysteries we'd picked up en route. Carbine offered a bill from a Chicago barber —

hair cut — 45 cents

shampoo — 15 cents

blackheads removal — 23 cents

nostril hairs — 17 cents

Total to be settled — $1

Eddie Booth produced a London Underground ticket
from the day
we entered the earth like moles
at Waterloo
to re-emerge at a place
called Shepherd's Bush.
One by one we had come up to street level
straightening ties, re-setting our caps.
Between Waterloo and Shepherd's Bush
we'd temporarily left the world
and McGregor and Gillett had checked their timepieces
until Mister Dixon confirmed that time
had indeed marched on.
We shared out tobacco and gathered round to exchange lists of
'firsts' —
the Negro shiphand on the SS *Rimutaka*
the Atlantic as seen in naval paintings
afternoon tea that time 376 feet up the Eiffel Tower
meeting the King at the Royal Cattle Show and Bubs Tyler shaking his
hand
French latrines
promenading (Jimmy's word) in the Gallery of Battles at Versailles
Carbine's wind-assisted monster field goal against Swansea
the music grinder outside Paddington Station with his shirt open to a
chest tattoo: Jesus RIP
the cruel metal spikes on the rafters at Paddington Station to
discourage pigeons from roosting
ice hockey
a Turkish bathhouse in Chicago
the 'suicides' propped up in chairs at the Paris morgue
the dappled giraffe led by a man in a turban past the smouldering
bonfires of the circus's camp in Putney
the farcical acts of the Italian Circus: jugglers fumbling tea cups, and
time and again the soaring acrobat missing the outstretched hands

of the red-nosed clown

We crossed the Nevada desert
climbed down the Grand Canyon
searched for old Indian arrowheads
traversed the Rockies
wound in and out of fruit orchards and cornfields
and after six days and seven nights on the train
in Port Richmond we boarded a ferry
and shipped across the bay to a city
back-lit by a bejewelled light.

We toured Chinatown,
a Chinese boot factory
soaked in saltwater baths at the Olympic Club.

At Berkeley, the authorities ploughed up a perfectly good playing field
in the mistaken belief that the game conditions required mud . . . and
at the last minute we switched the contest to a nearby baseball field
where we twice beat All-British Columbia before a crowd of fifteen
hundred, including newspapermen —

'. . . there were plenty of plays that could be styled brilliant. Long runs,
with difficult passes at just the moment when the runner was tackled,
made the exhibition more than a pretty sight to see. It was beautiful . . .'

We'd left Harper and Glenn in London. They had chosen to tour the
continent before sailing home via Suez. We left Seeling in London to
nurse Massa Johnston who was too sick to travel. In Frisco we shed
two more players. A ship's doctor said Freddy Roberts was in too bad a
way to continue. Mister Dixon asked for a volunteer to stay behind to
nurse Fred and Billy Wallace stuck up his hand.

A doctor in the city had cut out Fred's tonsils without anaesthetic. And Fred, though he didn't complain, hadn't reacted all that well. His weight dropped to nine stones. He couldn't eat, drink or talk. He couldn't raise himself out of bed. Fred didn't care where he was for the time being so long as no one moved him. It scared Billy Wallace half to death just to look at him. Fred's white face. His raw throat bled into the third day. Billy stood at the door asking Fred if he could do anything. Poor Fred had to shake his head on his pillow, and as he did so, the blood leaked and dribbled from the corner of his mouth, a bright red trickle of a kind that caused Billy to stand straighter and take his hands out of his pockets.

To show Fred there's nothing to be alarmed about he begins to reminisce. 'Hey Fred, remember that dive you did off the upper deck of the ship at Tenerife? You're lucky to be here at all. Lucky to be alive, mate. And that's the God-honest truth . . .' Fred manages a smile. He's turned his head to the wall, and Billy thinking that he's delivered Fred to the sunny harbour at Santa Rosa, murmurs into the dusky light this final thought: 'Sunshine, pineapples and whatnot . . .' and closes the door.

Out in the street the afternoon fog is rolling in from Ocean Beach. Already he has that local knowledge; like in London, always knowing the whereabouts of Hyde Park, and in Paris the river; in New York sticking to Broadway and looking for the straw boaters; here, in San Francisco, city of light, it is the fog that turns his head in the direction of Ocean Beach. The busy sidewalk pedestrian traffic parts either side of him. Women with happy flowers in their black bonnets look to either side, none with a spark of interest in him. So this is what it's like to be a nobody in an unfamiliar city. He could be anyone. Why, he could be a Polish Count. He smiles at that thought, and at the thought of the boys carousing south on the Sonoma, and thinks how scattered they've become. Billy Glenn and Eric Harper in Egypt by now, gazing up at the pyramids. Massa Johnston and Seeling in London. He pictures Massa in his sickbed, his bored face staring at the pale London sky in the window pane, drifting in and out, waiting for Bronco to enter the room from the world of big movement and noise, a hot lemon drink breathing through its lace cover in his big dumb hands, that gash over his right eye.

He wonders if they will ever meet again.

In Jones Street, Billy Wallace climbs aboard the tram that'll run him out to Ocean Beach. He's told the boys he intends to 'see them off . . .' He's promised them that if he sees the ship stuck on the horizon he'll give the stern a little tap to free it on its way south. He had better do what he said he would do.

◆

At Pago Pago we were rowed ashore by the natives
The air was made up of banana and coconut — and
when Corbett idly mentioned the mud and bog at Middlesex
we strained to remember that world.

Cunningham played marathon games of draughts with a missionary. In the thick afternoon heat we listened to the click and snick of the draughts and Cunningham's clerical summing up — 'That's one hundred and thirty-five games to your hundred and thirty-three . . .' We'd see the missionary come out of the shade and blink in the dazzling light, and rest his hands on the ship rail to try and find resolve out to sea.

Now that we'd left the great continent behind we slid down the long sloping banks of the Pacific for home.

There were the usual shipboard games — skittles, quoits, cards. But we had given up deck running, blind boxing and pillow fights. We did nothing to improve our conditioning. We took to deckchairs and waited for home to show on the horizon. That was the life waiting for us. The other we'd left behind in Europe. We were somewhat betwixt, lame in our deckchairs, like old folk sharing memories.

We laid out our mementoes, our exotic trinkets, old match programmes, postcards in which we featured, newsclippings — this story we'd created for ourselves, this new idea of ourselves
We didn't have an exact word for it
not yet we didn't
but we thought we knew it when we saw it
and began to amass examples —
The closure of the Great Western Railway Workshops for the afternoon, in Gloucester, and for none of the traditional reasons, the funeral of a Royal, the marriage of a Royal, the Coronation of a new King or Queen, but to see 'us'

In West Wales, just before kick-off, rainclouds had come no farther than the river

The afternoon the birds around Crystal Palace retired from the air, content to sit and watch when the silver ferns took the field

The French, delirious with joy, celebrating their first try with headstands, handsprings, Catherine wheels and somersaults

In Oxford, the scholars stood dazzled by the new design and form of play that came and went, like rare speech describing new concepts heard once and never after repeated

The request of the small paralysed boy to George Smith to sign his name over his dead limbs

At Blackfriar, a beggar girl selling matches running to light Jimmy Duncan's pipe

overseas experience

Up and down Elephant & Castle Bridge unsainted women lifting their skirts to offer themselves

The marriage proposal to Smithy with the caveat — 'if not him, then one of the other backs'

Arriving to the ground at Lansdown Road to find touts selling five shilling tickets for 45 shillings

A professional wizard, a predicter of fortunes, a seer, and three witches were driven out of town following the Irish defeat at Lansdown Road

The English shoeshine manufacturer's brilliant new brand — 'All Black Nugget'

The way the New York skyline appeared out of the sea mist, highly charged, knowing, in anticipation of travellers with new tricks

The shoving match between chaffeurs outside the hotel in Paris for the right to drive Gallaher, Duncan and Mister Dixon to Parc des Princes

Applause! Applause! Wave after wave of it

The quiet applause of the dazed Leicester players walking back to their goal line after conceding another try

The night Annette Kellerman interrupted her 100th performance of the 'Lady Champion Swimmer' to introduce Gallaher, Stead and Billy Wallace to the rest of the audience at the London Hippodrome

The two old country women who recognising their faces gave Gillett and Harper a basket of hard-boiled eggs for free

The Duke of Portland's gift to Billy Wallace, a number of chestnut hairs from the tail of Carbine, winner of the Melbourne Cup in 1890

The 35,000 telegrams sent out by the Cardiff Post Office following our only defeat at Cardiff Arms (normal Saturday load: 800 messages)

Declaration of a public holiday the day Hartlepool met us on the field

Birds in Cardiff falling from the sky hopelessly disoriented by the fifty thousand singing 'Men of Harlech'

French girls running alongside our cars, shouting, and holding up the hems of their dresses, following victory at Parc des Princes

Five shilling tickets selling for five quid the day of the match against England

Entering the New Brighton Theatre and the audience rising to their feet to cheer and demand a haka

Calling cards from Madame Tussaud placed under the doors of Carbine, Jimmy Hunter, and Dave Gallaher

At Taunton, sunlight catching the white throats of the largest crowd ever to see a match in Somerset

The non-verbal humility of world strongman Eugene Sandow and his assistants studying us in our baths following victory over Middlesex

◆

Heading the bill at Crystal Palace, Dec 2, 1905
roller skating in the centre transept
David Garrick Theatre 4 pm & 8 pm

overseas experience

Leoni Clarke's Cats, 3.30 pm, 5 pm, & 7.30 pm
Hire Wire Act noon & 1.15
NEW ZEALAND v ENGLAND 3 pm

Inside the magnificent Crystal Palace, China and Tunisia shared a
pavilion, Persia was lumped with Asia, while we were given the whole
field on which to display our conventions and ideas

'Vous êtes l'homme, Stead, oui?' *A stranger turning round from the Venus*
de Milo in Paris

'The way the New Zealanders conquer space . . .' *The artist in*
conversation with a reporter from the Figaro *on his new Cubist manifesto*

The staunch refusal of potato sellers under the archways of the
London Tower to accept payment for their baked potatoes

Gallaher & O'Sullivan munching baked potatoes by the river and filthy
pick-pocketing urchins keeping a respectful distance, and for the first
time in their short lives sensing 'fair game' out of bounds

To take the field and know already, like highwaymen, the shape of
future events

Those to whom the inexplicable attaches itself —
defeat to Wales
the crowing of witches in the Cardiff fog

The street fights that broke out for printed fliers promoting a biscuit
manufacturer's brand with a photo of the team

The proud Welsh adopting our ways for the match at Cardiff Arms

Following a visit by Nicholson & Stead the sudden and overwhelming demand for boots made under the Empress brand by the Midlands firm of Kempton, Stevens & Co

Our being the first party to have the privilege of a reserved car on the Metropolitan line en route to Oxford

The red-bitten fingers of the autograph hunters waiting with their bits of paper in the cold for our arrival at Folkestone

For the first time in the streets around Headingly the hawkers of bananas were outnumbered by vendors of 'All Black cards'

The reserving of seats for the players near the choir for 'divine service' in Westminster Abbey

Every colliery in the Forest of Green closing on the day we played Gloucester

In Hartlepool when shops and schools closed, the roofs around the ground were black with spectators, the top of the fort was blue with artillerymen, and enthusiasts climbed to the top of the lighthouse to catch our style

Achieving the biggest gate in Gloucester's history

The afternoon we paid a visit to Rectory Field and the Albion and Torquay players stopped play and joined the general spectator mêlée swarming towards us

In South Wales where we were compared to tea leaves: '. . . the New Zealanders have won great fame! Maypole Tea has done the same!' And toffees too: 'Like the New Zealand team, Turners cream caramel toffee is carrying all before it.'

Our appearance on a poster for Jason's Underwear. 'It may interest you to know that Jason Underwear has given general satisfaction to many members of the New Zealand footballers . . .'

Glasgow feeling sick and someone opening the window for him to dunk his head into the second floor air — and from afar came the sound of the Welsh victory hymn.

The creation of moments never forgotten:
'Suddenly I had the field to myself . . .' *Durham's P Clarkson recalls the first try scored against us for the newspapermen*

And, 'Hunter dived, dodged, and twisted clean through practically all the opposing side within twenty yards of his own line. It was a splendid meteoric flash, and fairly held the ranks of Richmond dumb . . .'

The *London Illustrated News* compares our crusade to the outcome of the Russo–Japanese War: '. . . and even the New Zealanders' merry victories in the mud suffer the very canker that slew the interest in the war. They are so uniformly one-sided . . .'

Our defeat at Cardiff Arms marking the 'beginning of time in Wales'

'I never saw anything like it in my life. I was reminded of Rome in the ancient days.' *A spectator from the Continent speaking to a* Western Mail *reporter the day after the Cardiff Arms Test*

To become the legend of rumour —

'. . . the Music Hall manager who gets the New Zealanders to walk across his stage at Drury Lane . . .' And, '. . . the politician who kicks off in a match in which [the New Zealanders] are beaten will be certain of a seat at the next General Election.'

The sudden feeling of elevation, a lightness underfoot, quick appreciation all around

Readiness on the part of others to laugh or smile at the slightest thing said

The suspension of judgement

❖

Three days south of Apia the air was less sultry. Still warm, but thinner — thin enough for some of us to scent the hills and ranges over which this air had shifted.

Two days before we sighted Northland, Jimmy Hunter picked up the scent of hill country. He leant over the rail, his nose set in the direction of land, his nostrils flared — 'That's a heifer,' he says. 'And that . . . well that's just a sheep. A flock of them . . .' And later that afternoon: 'I believe that's a dairy herd. Probably Jersey, if I'm not mistaken . . .'

At night we gathered on deck beneath the Southern Constellation. 'Our arrangement,' noted Mister Dixon. 'Our sky.'

March 5, 1906, we lined the deck to stare at the distant coast — it lay almost flat to the level of the sea — and each man's face contained his domestic situation.

❖

The next morning we were back at the rail to watch the country slide past.

The low-slung hills.

The whiff of tidal areas wrenching from us ancient memories.

At the appearance of small houses with space around them we thought of the different kinds of knowledge we'd come into —

meeting the King at the Royal Agricultural Show and seeing the easy way he handled strangers

the private entertainment of thoughts on the faces of women when parting company with their menfolk

the things you see but can never tell about

the different ways women had of touching: the crisp gloved hand versus the brush of a bare forearm

the different colours of a woman's face: the rose daubed on her cheek
to the welling up of colour from forbidden places

the way a woman's saying 'Pleased to make your acquaintance' could
be a great deal less exciting than her saying nothing at all; how eyes
could take over at such a moment

the things you could never talk about again

the quickening of blood that time in Montmarte when a woman
stepped from a doorway and opening her coat revealed her nakedness,
and how Frank G refused to act surprised, the way he closed both hands
over his cigarette, its glow capturing his grin before the door closed
and darkness returned

◆

Where the coast broke the *Sonoma* took a right-hand turn and we
followed the Gulf waters through to the harbour with Tyler, Gallaher
and Nicholson competing to name various points in the neigh-
bourhood.

A lightness overcame us. We felt silly as kids. Casey pinched Tyler's
hat and was about to toss it overboard when Mister Dixon caught his
eye with a quick and irritable look and Casey handed Tyler his hat
back.

A verse of song came to Nicholson. 'Hall lay lewya, Hallelujah,
Hallelujah, Hallylaylewohhaohhya.'
Corbett socked a fist in the palm of his hand.
God knows why but O'Sullivan had a sudden urge to draw a line with
a make-believe firearm and shoot at a big white stationary cloud.
George Gillett clucked his tongue and nodded with general approval.
Hunter, Deans & Co hugged the rail like it was a stock fence.
Only Jimmy Duncan remained quizzical, like it might be a trick, an
apparition; it might really be Tenerife with its open sewers and
Spaniards. Jimmy adopted a side-on position as if desirous of the

crowd's credentials and intentions before further committing himself.

In the near distance, we could see thousands upon thousands of people crammed on to the wharves. Others had taken advantage of the rooftops. Mister Dixon removed his hat then put it back on.

People in tiny sailing boats swarmed around us. They stood to wave, one hand on the tiller. They cried out our names. They shouted their welcome. Kia ora. The seagulls swooped and squawked. Kia ora. The green water splashed and turned white with boats. A small tug plied its way out to us. Word passed along that it was the Premier. Mister Dixon adjusted his necktie. He coughed in Corbett's direction and nodded at the tongue of shirt hanging out the back of his trousers. Nicholson was bursting to do a haka and had to be constrained. Jimmy Duncan blinked. He tried his hands on his hips, then went back to his previous position. The tug pulled alongside and we saw Seddon, big and heavy-footed, feel his way across the gangway. He seemed to fall into Mister Dixon's arms. Mister Dixon stood him up and clasped his arms. Seddon beamed out in all directions. He saw Gallaher and went to clasp him. Then he saw Stead and went in his direction. Then he took in Jimmy Hunter and Sully and Corbett. 'Boys. Boys. Boys.' He said to Deans, 'You must be Deans.' Eventually he reached us all. He got to the end and looked around. 'I don't see Billy Wallace.' Then he began to name those who were still wending their way home. Freddy Roberts. Bill Glenn. George Seeling. Massa Johnston. Eric Harper. Mister Dixon explained the situation and the Premier nodded good-naturedly and with a twinkling of understanding in his eyes. Then he roared at us, 'How did you like America?' America was good, we said. Big. Vast. Busy. Full of people. Interesting landscape. Then someone had the sense to say, 'Not as good as home,' and the Premier roared at us and in the direction of the thousands down at the wharf: 'Did you hear that? Did you hear that!'

In single file, we carried our hand luggage down the gangway to cheering and applause. It was a different kind of applause to that which we were used to. It was applause people did when what they really

overseas experience

wished to do was hug you. In Europe the applause had been respectful, sharp, voluminous, but quickly over; at other times a long slow clap that bordered on fatigue at yet another trick displayed.

A huge wagon and horses were waiting for us. We climbed up on the wagon and took our seats. People reached up to shake our hands. Then as we moved off a cheer rose up Queen Street where still thousands more gathered. Ours was the only vehicle. The only wagon in Queen Street. The people cheered, and it got to where sitting was an insufficient gesture. We stood and waved our hats at the crowd. We heard our names rise and fall like a confetti loosened over the city.

◆

That night we attended our official home-coming dinner:

Ox Tail Soup

Clear Turtle Soup

✤

Fried Flounder

✤

Poulet à la Mango

Roast Duckling

Roast Suckling Pig & Apple Sauce

Kumara, French Beans

✤

Trifle

Champagne

Marashira & Macedonian Jellies

ORCHESTRA NUMBERS

'Santiago'

'Sea Songs'

'Road to Moscow'

'Rowsy Dowsy Girls'

Over the course of the dinner and between songs we entertained those around us with accounts of the amazing things we'd seen. They wanted to know what the King was like, were the French hospitable? clean? and the women? 'Oh la la . . .' Really? 'Oh, la la . . .' What about black people? Spaniards? Yes . . . No . . .? they'd heard . . . Quite nice, are they? Civil? Good. That's good. Our audience was relieved. They sat back and patted their lips with the stiff white napkins. We described taking afternoon tea inside the 'eye' of the huge wooden elephant on the Coney Island shore, and skyscrapers so tall that at night stars appeared to rest on top; we talked about shooting molly-hawks from the stern of the boat off Uruguay and described the huge swimming pool at Montevideo, all enclosed, with 220 dressing rooms, and the Turkish baths and 'hot air baths' and douches taken at San Francisco's Olympic Club. And from Jimmy Duncan to the game's commissars some campaign matters: 'Thompson broke down on three separate occasions, Abbott poisoned a leg, Smithy busted his ribs, Massa's sick as a dog, in hospital when we last heard, Tyler did his ankle, McDonald and Casey did their shoulders, Sully broke his collarbone, Roberts lost his tonsils, Mackrell was sick from day one, for a while McDonald had his arm in a sling. . .and boils, don't ask me about boils. . .'

overseas experience

Billy Stead is the last one home. Boarding the *Arawa* at Onehunga, he thinks, 'What if, what if there is no homecoming? What if, like Odysseus, home is always on the horizon?' Then he smiles to himself, relieved that no one heard that thought.

Sailing on to New Plymouth and Wanganui, disembarking briefly in Wellington for a banquet, speeches, toasts. Then out to sea again, sliding in and out of the country, sitting on starboard, knees crossed, grimacing back at the great folded land . . . close-up views, views from afar, everything in place, as remembered, cherished, everything as it should be.

Plumbing a stranger's thoughts by the way he happens to stand with a shovel against himself while rolling a smoke

or the heart of a crowd by the way the eyes pitch, sunshine at their rear, knowing fame's ciphers

experiencing the comings and goings of insight, and all over again the thrill of noting how at a glance the mountains can suck up all knowledge and render you speechless.

On to Dunedin, another banquet. There is just this one to get through. The tributes. The expressions of gratitude. The backslapping city officials. The singing of the anthem, eyes tilted to the ceiling, followed by more toasts. 'Ladies and gentlemen, charge your glasses and please be upstanding . . .' and rising again on his sore knees with his glass in hand.

And finally, on horse and dray cantering in to a big welcome home in Invercargill; by now knowing the drill, grinning at the ground at the feet of the crowd, moving instinctively into that space cleared for him to make his way to the podium, glancing away to avoid the nervous, besotted look of the Mayor. For perhaps the hundredth time hearing 'Ladies & gentlemen . . .' He glances up and casts his eye over the crowd of faces, many of them friends, family, strangers some, and those to the rear, figures from childhood standing with folded arms and guarded faces. He will be expected to speak. There's no escaping that. This is why all these people are here, to see and hear him. But what to say? What can be said that adequately captures everything that needs to be said? There are so many competing thoughts, so many textures and varieties of thought. Billy settles on one face. The man is smiling back as if Billy should know him — long cheekbones like those pillars of light the clouds cast down over Tuatapere Plain. Hmm. Billy smiles and the stranger smiles back. A woman cries out — 'Say something Billy . . .' There is so much to say. So much that is there in his thoughts. So much to retrieve. Suddenly his thoughts are back in the Latin Chapel in Oxford. The good people of Invercargill look up and see him smiling. Billy smiling — they are glad for that at least. But what they can't see is what Billy is smiling at. Bob Deans is directing his attention to a magnificent stained glass window, to its 'ship of souls journeying from the world to Heaven.' Deans's words, his version. The restlessness of the crowd draws him back to the moment at hand. One or two call out —

'Can't hear you . . .'

'Come on, Billy . . . Say something to us . . . Give us some words.'

A light rain begins to fall but not a single umbrella reveals itself. Look how the turned-up faces grow shiny. Then, horrifying him as it happens, his thoughts skate off to Paris, to the Venus de Milo. There is no logic in his disembodied self. But he goes with the thought for the few seconds it takes. He and the excitable Cooks man are at the Louvre and Billy's just asked after the Aphrodite's missing limb. The way the shoulder is twisted: he has an idea she might have held something and the Cooks man is able to confirm this. Aphrodite had held a mirror in her hand. A gift from Alexandros, the sculptor, her maker. 'So,' he says, 'she could see for herself how she had been entirely shaped out of the desire of another.'

And that's it, of course. The connection made, Billy smiles. His lips part and instantly the crowd falls quiet. Their faces go still. This is the moment they have come for. They are surprised by the smallness of his voice and the obviously tired corner from which it has roused itself.

'Thank you,' says Billy Stead. 'Thank you for everything.'

◆

For the record, we scored 830 points and conceded 39.

eight

off the record

eight

Einstein and Matisse caused a stir
that year
Freud came later
They brought to the surface
hitherto unseen worlds
Dreams, inner truth
the essence of things
and, applied to them —
names
colour
formulae

We introduced new ideas to Europe
The 2,3,2 scrum formation
The wing forward, 'controversial'
but effective
A fullback who played with a sun hat on
and ran outside the wing —
in themselves, perhaps they're not much
but the thought — the thought is what counts
Back yourself
Give it a go
Anticipate

Draw
Back up
Re-invent
Challenge
Change

People flocked to see us
as they did
the African pygmies
sword-swallowing Moroccans
the bloated Japanese carp
and Annette Kellerman
at the London Hippodrome

We were up there
with Asia and floating icebergs
a thing of wonder

We who had come to discover
found ourselves discovered
and, in the process, discovered
ourselves —
the solemn faces of Newton and Corbett and the nervousness of their hands whenever dinner plates were set before them
McDonald's dainty way of drying himself, first towelling his feet, then each toe — not something you ordinarily see in a big man
the break-through day that saw huge, uncomplaining George Nicholson send his runny eggs back to the kitchen in Glasgow (how we cheered!)
Cunningham's love of shovelling coal into the stoker of the SS *Rimutaka*
Seeling's refusal to do the same
that time outside Oxford, walking in on Bob Deans alone in the chapel, and Bob turning, quick as you like, to introduce the saints, making it

clear a friend of his was a friend of yours, astonished that you hadn't
met before

O'Sullivan's ability to bump through almost any opposition

cheery Freddy Roberts singing 'Have I got a girl for you' to lift our
spirits while we stood about in the sleet and rain waiting for the
Durham boys to take the field

the hacking cough of poor Mackrell at night and his willingness to
play

Steve Casey giving up the chance of a try in Paris in order to preserve
his try-less record

off the record

Getting to know one man's preference for a bed by the window
and another's need for the seat in the aisle, thank you

Those who preferred black tea with one sugar, and those who take it
with milk, and no sugar

the early nighters

the insomniacs

the sleepwalker whose big toe had to be tied by cotton thread to the
bed post

Those who could be relied upon in a crisis (George Smith's heroics at
Inverleith come to mind)

and those who were prepared to do things differently (Glasgow kicking
a conversion out of the mud by placing the ball sideways like a log of
wood)

The impulse of some to stop and pat a mangy dog

and the single-minded haste of others

But mostly
the knowledge gained
was something more or less
inexact
a feeling
of shape & movement
that understanding of trees in a high wind

of knowing what to do
having been there before & all that
The simplest of ideas gained & held on to
from things
that move together
in a loose shambling way — or
what others like to call
harmony

As Billy Stead once said, 'There are moral advantages from combination . . .' For instance —

the time at a hoi polloi dinner that Carbine forgot the word he was searching for & George Smith chimed in
beautifully
with a connected subject

In Limerick, the folded note intended for George Smith from the wealthy Irish widow passing through three sets of safe hands — McDonald's, Casey's and Bronco Seeling's

The selfless way of Deans, Harper and Hunter dipping into their own deeper pockets each Monday to pool together a couple of quid for one of their less well-off team mates

Mister Dixon clearing his throat when 'Hokitika' Corbett picked up the dessert spoon as the soup was being served

The silky intervention of Bill Glenn, again at Limerick, when O'Sullivan surrounded by Irish loosies was asked for his opinion on the 'Irish question'

The tact and experience of Mister Dixon when Johnston came downstairs without a trouser belt and, on another occasion, in the gents of the Trocadero nuggeting George Tyler's trouser belt to match his dinner suit

The writing of fake love letters to those who missed out

The 'Taipu move' in which Jimmy Hunter props inside his opposite and flicks the ball back on his inside; the idea that space can be wooed

Mynott's cry of 'My try, Jimmy' and Jimmy Hunter, after running through half the Bedford team, handing the ball on

That moment in Tenerife when pigeons flew out the church doors and Jimmy O'Sullivan had the presence of mind to say, 'On a wing and a prayer . . .'

Smithy mopping Sully's brow and nursing his temperature down from 105°F aboard the *Rimutaka*

Mackrell sick with influenza staying behind in Tyemouth to nurse Bunny Abbott with his poisoned leg

The way one man's view and joys complemented another's —
the contrasting delights found in the British Library
For Stead: a letter by Lord Nelson outlining his strategy for Trafalgar
For Deans: 'The Codex Sinaiticus' or as he told Glasgow 'The Bible in Greek'

The way one man filled in a piece of the world unknown to the other —
Nicholson and Stead bootmakers
Gallaher a freezing worker
Billy Wallace a foundryman
Corbett a miner
Deans, Hunter and Harper farmers

Bunny Abbott a professional runner and farrier
Glasgow a bank officer
Mona Thompson a civil servant, and so on . . .

There had been others —
one thinks of Roman galleys
pulling on oars out to the wide ocean
The Crusaders come to mind
And those in sailing ships
peeking around hillsides of ice

Worlds bound by the same elemental fear & wonder.

◆

So what of memory? What sticks?

Thirty years after the tour ends, invited to write a piece of reminiscence
Billy Stead recalls the winding lanes of Devon, the secret stairways of
Holyrood, the dank corridors of the Tower of London, the dust particles
that hung in the air of a celebrated dressmaker's shop in Paris, and
that terrible night outside Cherbourg taking on emigrants from the
French tender 'four in a basket . . . and shot down an incline on to the
lower deck (just like the mail).' It is an older Billy Stead writing, re-
evaluating, reflecting.

He recalls Gallaher travelling all the way south to Reefton to tell him
he's signed up for the war in Europe. Another campaign. Just the two
of them this time, they sat on a rock at the edge of a field, trailing
thoughts. In the near distance, two lovers, a boy and a girl, stood by
the ruins of an old well: the boy with rolled-up shirt sleeves gamely
letting down the bucket, and she — closing her eyes to make a wish,
and Billy thinking — 'Everyone seeks the future.'

With regards to the future that's another story —
Gallaher with his head shattered by an exploding shell
Harper picked off by a sniper in Palestine
The poisoned appendix that saw poor Deans shovelled into the ground
at 23 years of age
One by one, we were tapped on the shoulder by our Maker

In 1955, those of us still alive gathered at Athletic Park for the camera
McDonald is coated up, his hands pinned behind his back
O'Sullivan on canes
Nicholson, a silver fern on his lapel, tall, erect as an Anzac morning
veteran
Billy Stead perky around the mouth, but surely his ears have grown
Bunny Abbott with his hat held inside out
Fats Newton on canes, elegantly bulked up
Gillett's shorn off his moustache & lost his film star looks to the inflated
dimensions of a successful small town lawyer; a timepiece is sewn in
his midriff
Freddy Roberts looks pin sharp in an elegant dark coat
Billy Wallace looks intact

After that, the picture begins to fade
to a crowded city bar on Lambton Quay
two old men driven into a smoky corner
unnoticed
by rowdy young men with long wild hair, platform shoes, flared
trousers and coloured beads

And then? Well it happens that
all the old protagonists are dead.
Seddon who spoke fine words in 1906
rises in a massive column at the entrance to Bowen Street Cemetery
A seagull perches on his shoulder leaving its scatological package

off the record

The crowds that filled the wharves and Queen Street have gone
Crowds in Cardiff, Crystal Palace, Edinburgh, Paris, across America
all are gone. Dead. Buried. Silent.

For a period after, memory drifted
in and out of plans to build altars
but nothing ever came of them.
Across the country's playing fields
you saw men with their hearts and mouths open
while myth sat in its cave
knees drawn up, eyelids closed.

THE BOOK OF FAME

afterthoughts

'Our attitude [to individualism] is one of unofficial and very guarded approval.'
Billy Stead in The Complete Rugby Footballer

'The exhibition given by the New Zealanders surpassed in individual and collective merit anything previously seen . . .'
Western Daily Press

'There are moral advantages from combination as apart from actual ones, as, for instance, when a player is making a great and difficult individual effort and is closely attended during this risky period by a trusty colleague ready to take the ball from him at the moment that his own possession of it becomes untenable.'
The Complete Rugby Footballer

'The quickest road to fame is to play the New Zealanders.'
Football News

'Com-e-dy, com-e-dy, siss, boom, brek-e-kex, aouei, whee!'
A phonetic rendering of the haka by an American newspaper reporter for his readers

'. . . his nose for a gap and sense of timing created a path from boot maker to Prince . . .'
Gallaher's fake obituary for Stead written at the 'dime obituary tent' on a visit to Dreamland on Coney Island in 1906

Insults to consider:

Durham keeping us out in the sleet for 30 minutes before taking the field

the refusal of the Scots to grant their players 'caps' for the game against us

their decision to dine alone after the match

& their ungracious demand that we supply the ball

haggis, nothing but haggis

the shabby trick of the Welsh to drag Deans back from the try-line after he scored

the shifting sideline beneath the straw that denied Dunk McGregor his try against Swansea

the statement of accounts following the match against Blackheath: gross gate 760 pounds less expenses 300 pounds, that included 'Lunch for the New Zealand team, 27 pounds! for a cold dish or two'

the drafting of internationals into the Bedford playing XV which included only 6 bona fide Bedford men

the questionable invitation from the English Union to have the team properly tailored in coats and blazers after the style of the English . . .

acknowledgements

'We began with myths and later included actual events.' This charming line appears in Michael Ondaatje's book of poems, *Handwriting*. *The Book of Fame* proceeds along similiar lines. The myth of the 1905 Originals precedes this novel, as do various match reports on the games played. Actual events outside of the matches, however, have been harder to come by and where obtainable not that interesting or even illuminating. This is where the imagination slips easily into the gaps. While this book is a work of the imagination it is nonetheless bedded in research. I spent one May in England visiting the old playing fields in Camborne, Exeter, and in Wales, as well as many, many hours holed up in the British Newspaper Library combing the brittle and yellow pages of the period. Where possible I tried to follow in the footsteps of the Originals; at the County Ground where Gallaher's men played their opener I found the field, turnstiles, and surrounding vista of chimney pots and cycle track unchanged; though altered in this respect: a young man was coaching a woman's rugby team. In Newton Abbot I found the Globe Hotel converted to a drapery, though the hotel columns and the watchtower outside are still intact. In Taunton the hotel that accommodated the team is now a wonderful bookshop. Another of the team's hotels, the Great Western outside Paddington, is in the throes of renovation. In Cardiff, the Queen's Hotel still stands across the road from the old Cardiff Arms Park, and is a bare-boarded haunt of the local fans. Closer to home, many hours were spent in the tiny kitchen of the Rugby Museum in Palmerston North combing through players' mementoes and Billy Wallace's album. I am tremendously grateful to the Rugby Museum's Bob Luxford for both his interest and professional help in locating material and for keeping me topped up with tea and biscuits. Similiarly I want to thank Ron Palenski for lending me his copy of George Dixon's diary, a blow-by-blow account of the matches played on tour; and the staff at the Hocken Library who unearthed Billy Stead's scrapbooks. I would also like to thank my agent Michael Gifkins and publisher Geoff Walker.

THE CURATIVE

Charlotte Randall

The narrator of this compelling and unusual novel is an inmate of Bedlam, the London mental asylum. He is living chained to a wall in unspeakably horrible conditions, yet he is witty, urbane and seemingly sane. He reflects on freedom, on love and on love lost, and on the fleeting nature of happiness.

As this beautifully constructed story unfolds we learn about the bizarre treatments he has endured under the asylum's curative regimen, his life before Bedlam, and the answers to the critical questions: *Why is this man here? What has he done?*

This novel deftly explores the devious in human affairs and the intricacies of language to create a brilliant and utterly memorable book.

Charlotte Randall's first novel, *Dead Sea Fruit* (1995), won both the Reed Fiction Award and Best First Book in the Asia/Pacific section of the Commonwealth Writers' Prize.

CITY OF REEDS
Tina Shaw

They are the Purefoy girls, three sisters who grow up safely in small-town New Zealand and then leave. Beth travels impulsively to Afghanistan; Clare becomes a doctor and goes to San Francisco; only Louise stays home and makes money.

But living safely can have hidden hazards.

Clare comes home, running away from the dangers of a disastrous love affair and immediately falls into another relationship.

Louise walks a fragile line between conventional life and the need to take risks, often of a sexual nature.

Beth is haunted by images of violence.

As Clare sifts through childhood memories, she realises that certain events have damaged them all. Will the Purefoy girls survive?

An exhilarating and moving story about family secrets, loss and reconciliation.

Tina Shaw is a 1999 Buddle Findlay Sargeson Award fellow, along with Kapka Kassabova. She has won several writing awards including the *Sunday Star Times* Short Story Competition.

RECONNAISSANCE

Kapka Kassabova

Nadejda is backpacking around New Zealand, in the surreal haze of summer. Her encounters are comic and revealing – and often sexual. But Nadejda's tour is a deep and personal one; it is a journey into memory and family myth.

Faded memories of happy times conflict with more disturbing pictures as her determination to uncover the truth is diffused with an immigrant's yearning to belong and a young woman's longing for love. And who is the mystery narrator who 'talks' to Nadedja as her travels lead her to him?

Set against the turmoil of present-day Bulgaria and the sweet simplicity of her new country, *Reconnaissance* is a grand, sweeping novel of family secrets, dislocation and ultimate reconciliation.

A powerful and sensual debut novel. Winner of the Best First Book category for the 2000 Asia/Pacific region of the Commonwealth Writers' Prize, and finalist in the 1999 Montana New Zealand Book Awards.

'Reconnaisance is a compelling, provocative novel which blends a coming-of-age story with the wider events of history.'

Virginia Were, *NZ Herald*

'Reconnaisance is a singular achievement: powerful, honest, brutal, erotic and assured.'

Graeme Lay, *North and South*

Talking about
O'Dwyer

C.K. Stead

What really happened when a soldier in the Maori Battalion was killed in action in the battle for Crete during the Second World War?

And why did the soldier's family place a makutu, a curse, on Donovan O'Dwyer, the Pakeha officer who was there when he died?

Half a century later old friends gather at the funeral of O'Dwyer, now an Oxford don. It is revealed that he spent half his life under the curse because it had been said that he killed one of his own men. As the narrative unfolds, so does the story of Mike Newall, a New Zealander living in Oxford, whose whole life has been touched in vital ways by these events.

This powerful new novel by C. K. Stead is about war and peace — and about the points of friction, and of enrichment, where different cultures and traditions intersect and overlap. It is Stead at his finest.

Classical
Music
JOY COWLEY

We dive together and come up, our clothes floating around us. The water is surprisingly warm and it occurs to me that this is the first time we've been in the sea together since her near-drowning incident.

Delia and Bea, sisters, but never close. Delia lives a glamorous life in New York and Bea lives thousands of miles away in New Zealand, looking after elderly parents and playing the role of dutiful daughter. Delia and Bea both long for the warmth and intimacy of sisterhood, but it always eludes them.

When Delia rushes home for their father's funeral there is an opportunity to spend some time together, but Delia and Bea move in orbit around each other, both recalling grievances and hurts, neither prepared to admit their need for each other. But as the day of the funeral passes, memories are unlocked: memories of their mother and her passion for music, memories of their father and memories of a magical summer and a man they had all loved.

Joy Cowley is one of New Zealand's most loved children's writers. She is also famous all over North America for her wonderful children's readers. *Classical Music* is her second adult novel.

'This novel offers a sophisticated look at the present and a sensitive evocation of the past. It is Joy Cowley at her very best.'

Barbara Wall, *Timaru Herald*

LIVE
BODIES
Maurice Gee

'. . . *Live Bodies* is a stunningly effective and confident work of fiction. This may be Maurice Gee's best ever.'

Ian Richards, *NZ Listener*

As a young man in Vienna in the 1930s, Josef Mandl battles the Nazis on the streets of Vienna. Fleeing to New Zealand he is interned as a dangerous alien on Somes Island in Wellington harbour. After the war he becomes a successful businessman, a family patriarch. Now, in old age, he looks back, retracing his life.

I stepped out of one world and into another ...

'Gee has long been one of New Zealand's finest writers and his soaring strengths are in full evidence in *Live Bodies* ...'

Jenny Jones, *NZ Herald*

In *Live Bodies* Maurice Gee writes of loss and dispossession, of family, friendship and, most achingly, love. In this his finest book for years, his precise elegant prose cuts through their surface, investing even the familiar with touching significance.